To Wendy. With healing, love + blessings Shimara ♡

THE FLOWERS OF LIFE

FLOWER AND GEM ESSENCES FOR
HEALING AND SPIRITUAL TRANSFORMATION

by SHIMARA KUMARA

HEARTSONG PUBLICATIONS
PO Box 252
Totnes
Devon
TQ9 9DT
England

www.heartsong.eu

First printing 1997
New Edition 2018

ISBN: 978-0-9531533-3-6

The use of the material described in this book is not meant
to replace the services of a medical doctor who should
always be consulted for any condition needing medical help.

Cover photograph by Jeremy Opie

Typeset, printed and bound in Great Britain by
Short Run Press Ltd, Exeter, Devon

DEDICATION

This book is dedicated to the Soul who incarnated as Edward Bach, for the love, generosity of spirit and dedication to his Divine Mission in bringing back to the earth plane the remembrance of the healing power of flower essences.

WITH UNCONDITIONAL LOVE AND GRATITUDE FOR HIS DIVINE GIFTS TO HUMANITY.

ACKNOWLEDGEMENTS

My grateful thanks to all those who have been my teachers and guides in this life, for all I have learned and for any reflections you have given me to encourage my own clearing. My grateful thanks to the Ascended Masters for all their love and encouragement, particularly Sanat Kumara and Kuthumi. To Colin and Jeremy for their love and dedication in helping me over the many years, to create all the essences, healing systems and tools of light to help raise the consciousness of mankind. From my highest being I send unconditional love and reverence to Mother/Father God and to Mother Earth for the nurturing of the plant and mineral kingdoms and all the associated devas, fairies and light beings; without their love for humanity these essences would not exist.

It is delightful to have this book illustrated by such beauty and my grateful thanks go to the following people who have helped with this work by supplying such high quality photographs:

Grateful thanks to Dr. John Feltwell, Helmut Maier and Sam Cremnitz. Jeremy Opie for the beautiful cover photograph and many others.

LET US ALWAYS HOLD MOTHER EARTH IN LOVE AND LIGHT WITHIN OUR HEARTS TO HELP THIS PLANET ONCE AGAIN BECOME THE GARDEN OF EDEN.

CONTENTS

INTRODUCTION

This book is primarily about raising consciousness. In its pages you will find much information on the healing power of flower essences from several different systems, each having their own dosage instructions and duration of taking each of the frequencies. For this is what they are. If you can liken each emotion, mental pattern, thought, as being a certain vibrational frequency, as each carries its own subtle energy or vibration then you can start to have an understanding of some of the most fundamental laws of the Universe and how we are each creating in every moment energies around us and in fact, create our own reality. These can be seen by clairvoyants and sensitives as an energy field around each of our bodies. Through their eyes, each vibration has its own colour frequency related to the particular thoughts and beliefs we carry. For example the colour vibration of emerald green relates to the heart chakra, balance, harmony, unconditional love and the planet Venus, which exemplifies those qualities; interestingly, emerald gemstones were seeded on Earth from Venus aeons ago to help us carry that vibration in our hearts. The subtle energies we give off are not just the fantasies of psychics; they can now be seen to exist through the new technologies of kirlian/aura photography and electro-crystal therapy, in addition to the very latest advanced equipment used in the photographs in this book.

Obtaining a reading from one of these machines or a very skilled psychic, one can gain much information on oneself on many different levels, from imbalances and malfunction of physical organs or glands, to a lack of energy; and from the subtle vibrations of the chakra system and meridians we can see where the energy loss or imbalance is occurring. We are then able to be treated at causal level by the very fine, subtle frequencies of flower/gem essences, thus bringing us back to wholeness. We can also detect blockages in the subtle planes formed by unbalanced emotions and rigid mental patterns which cause difficulty at a personality level and transform them, bringing more joy into our lives. Therefore we can start to see that in future, medicine will be forced to look, not just at symptoms but at the causes of disease also, so that real healing can take place. The causes originate at subtle energy levels and can be tracked over a period of time by this new technology, or clairvoyantly, to the direct influence of the physical body through stress and ultimately to a breakdown of the more solid 3D vibrations (atoms and cells), which then causes disease or illness. As Edward Bach knew, dis-ease means simply a malfunction between the personality and soul, meaning not at ease. This ancient esoteric healing knowledge was known to all the wise ones and great souls such as Hippocrates, Paracelsus and Hanneman. This knowledge of harmony in the individual bringing health to the physical body has been lost in the modern world's race for materialism, intellectual knowledge and development of modern medicine which simply treats the symptoms. The fundamental belief structure underlying this form of treatment is that ill health is caused by outside forces, whereas the truth is that in some way we create our own experiences and illnesses by our negative beliefs, unbalanced emotions or poor lifestyle thus drawing negativity into the body through the subtle realms of thought down into dense matter. Change our thoughts and change our life! That's what flower essences do. There is no other form of medicine that helps us bring these permanent, positive changes so easily. These essences help us to live a happier, healthier life and raise our spiritual awareness to the levels necessary to birth the planet into her new consciousness, thus bringing peace to all humanity.

THE FLOWER ESSENCES DISCOVERED BY DR. EDWARD BACH

Dr. Edward Bach was a man of great courage and inner wisdom who became the "father" of flower essence therapy, just as Hanneman was the father of homeopathy, before him. Incarnated in 1886, he chose a family which would help him to develop certain qualities within his personality, as indeed each soul chooses before manifesting a physical body. His choice was a powerful father, helping him to develop his own strengths. The family business was a brass foundry and Edward's father was hoping his son would succeed him. Edward Bach however had higher visions, as he knew his Divine purpose was to serve humanity as a "healer" and from a very young age he had the sincere desire to become a doctor. His father would not yield to his son's requests so finally Edward Bach left school and went to train in his father's factory. His heart was not in it though, and eventually, under much pressure his father allowed him to leave and go to medical college. Already, Edward Bach was developing strength to stand up to those more powerful than himself for what he believed in, as we all need to do.

Edward Bach went on to become a brilliant doctor and bacteriologist discovering seven important nosodes which are still in use today. Recognising that allopathic medicine only treated the symptom and not the cause, his research eventually led him to train in homeopathy. As he treated his patients he became progressively more aware of the need to treat the personality to achieve any true healing, recognising that those patients of a very negative or emotional nature did not progress as well from their treatments as those of a more positive and balanced state of mind. A spiritual seeker of truth and healing, I feel that Edward Bach studied many different philosophies, religions and creeds. More and more he felt the truth of healing the personality imbalances would be found in nature with the flowers of the field that Mother/Father God had provided for us. Beginning to lose interest in his practice, he felt an inner calling to find new remedies which would help the individual to find hope, happiness, peace and purpose. Inner knowing told him, as did all the ancient doctrines, that as the personality felt better and became clearer, more balanced, so any disharmony (i.e. illness, disease), at a physical level would clear away. When the mind is more at one with the soul and soul's purpose, harmony comes to all levels of being, mind, body and spirit.

By 1929, Edward Bach had become a well respected doctor, researcher and immunologist, with a busy thriving practice in Harley Street. His peers and colleagues probably considered him quite insane when he announced his decision to leave the practice in the hands of others so that he could travel the countryside looking for a new system of healing from plants. The Divine path of Edward Bach was to discover the remedies for which he has now become famous. Each of us has a purpose, no matter how high or lowly; something to achieve in this lifetime which will benefit our fellow man. Unfortunately, most do not achieve this as they become blocked and unclear in their purpose, often ending their life in sadness with feelings of regret at their inability to find their true path. One of the most important remedies Edward Bach discovered was made from wild oat flowers and helps the individual to see where to go – the Divine Path. He knew that any healing power from plants would be more potent by utilising the help of all the elemental forces. Therefore, his discovery that dew drops held in a flower and potentised by the early morning sun could heal him when placed on his tongue, was the start of a grand, wonderful unfoldment; the re-discovery of flower essences.

As he wandered along the countryside looking for flowers to be used in his new system of medicine, Edward Bach would develop a certain mental or emotional pattern very strongly. So severe were these states that they often developed into physical ailments, proving to him that all illness is derived from thought patterns and emotions of one level or another. Edward Bach was a very spiritual and sensitive man and suffered severe mental and physical tortures during the process of finding and "proving" his new system of healing. It is obvious from the stories of this latter part of his life that he was a very clear "channel" for healing energy to come through, often healing with a touch of his hand. From a spiritual perception it seems that Edward Bach was a reincarnation of a very evolved soul, one which had developed these "gifts" in previous lifetimes. His sensitivity was so great that he could hold his hand over a flower and know its healing power. Indeed, this was how he was driven to alleviate each of the extreme states he suffered while discovering the remedies. After his discovery that the healing life force energy from a plant could be captured in dewdrops, he went on to create a method of making each flower essence in greater quantities. This was simply through using a pure glass bowl filled with spring water, then placing the blooms at the peak of their perfection on top and placing the bowl on the earth in full sunlight for 3-4 hours. Thus, he utilised the power of the five elements, earth, air, fire, water and ether. The healing power of plants has been known and used throughout history. All the ancients knew the secret lore of herbs. This knowledge was passed down traditionally through the family or tribe. Today we use homeopathy, herbalism and aromatherapy, each incorporating the healing energy in a different way. Flower essences, however, work in a more subtle way, yet very powerfully to help us become clearer.

38 different flower essences were discovered in total, each working to alleviate a different pattern within us. You could say that they cover all mental/emotional states known to man; any negative state we find ourselves in there is an essence which will flood us with the positive vibration, thus bringing harmony. During this process of discovery, Edward Bach suffered tremendously, mentally, emotionally and physically, to bring to mankind his gift of 38 healing essences.

Upon completion of his life's work, including establishing a system of dilution and trials conducted on new remedies to prove their efficiency, Edward Bach handed over his work to his dear friends and colleagues Nora Weeks and Victor Bullen. Entrusted to them was the task of spreading the knowledge of this new system of healing. Knowing he had completed his life's mission he peacefully left his body in his sleep and made the transition to become a spiritual guide on the higher dimensions – in our linear year 1936.

It was through his guidance and that of Victor Bullen, (who passed over much later, having given his life in service to his fellow man), that I was drawn to make all 38 flower essences. Often I would be guided to some of Edward Bach's original sites in Norfolk, where he lived for several years while discovering the essences. My first strong guidance came when I was searching a stream looking for water violet to make the essence. After two hours of walking and seeking I was very tired. I knew my instinct or inner guidance was telling me that this rare flower was in the area. As I sat on a log to meditate and try to locate it, I heard a man's voice very loudly and clearly telling me where to find it. The voice was so clear, I looked around but no one was there! Trusting, I followed the instructions and found the flowers. Afterwards, during meditation (which was then and still is a part of my everyday life), I spoke to this spiritual guide again and discovered Victor Bullen to be the dearest, most gentle man. His guidance came to me over the following years as I tried and tested the flower essences I made on patients, clients, and, as importantly, myself. Several clients who were mediumistic also described Victor, in perfect detail, when they saw his astral body in my consulting room. The essences proved to be extremely effective and soon other practitioners were asking if they could use them. This was the start of the company which has flourished under the guidance of the Ascended Masters and now provides the world with vibrational medicine.

All the flower essences are made strictly according to the original instructions of Dr. Edward Bach. As the essences are made we meditate with the plants, calling on the angelic realms and the flower devas to protect and bless the process. When the "mother" tinctures are made, we love and protect these subtle vibrations in glass bottles and amplify using sacred geometry. Our staff, who prepare the individual bottles, send out parcels and do the labelling (all by hand), work with love and care. No machinery is used in our process and the essences are EXACTLY as Dr. Edward Bach originally made them. The essences are NOT homeopathic dilutions but pure, high frequency, liquid light energy. All who work with us are healers in their own right and coming from a heart centred space and this is felt by so many who receive our essences.

HOW DO FLOWER ESSENCES HEAL?

There are many aspects to diagnosing and working with the 38 essences. The flowers are vibrational frequencies which are multi-dimensional in their healing power, often working in very subtle ways which, however, can bring profound change, healing and transformation to the individual. Here are just a few examples from my clients case studies, drawn from over 3 decades of work as a practitioner.

Flower remedies bring balance to the emotions

A patient came to see me feeling very unbalanced, irrational and suicidal. He had a past history of suicidal tendencies and had taken many anti-depressants, prescribed by his general practitioner over the years. I immediately gave him a glass of water with 2 drops of the essence Cherry Plum in it, and asked him to sip it every 5 minutes while we talked. At the end of the hour long consultation he was feeling much more balanced and positive. Using the essences in this way brings us back into balance quickly, in extreme states or emergencies. I then made him up 2 dosage bottles containing Cherry Plum and a few other essences he needed for long term states and prescribed 4 drops, 8 times a day. A few months later, after having stayed on Cherry Plum continually and having had several consultations, he stated that the deep rooted Cherry Plum irrational, emotional state had now completely disappeared. The essences had resolved a deep imbalance in his mind and he could now lead a full and happy life. This shows how the essences work on deep rooted states, healing long-standing issues.

Flower remedies help us to become calmer and less stressed with situations in life

One lady worked in a busy office and had a heavy workload. She would become very irritated because others did not work as fast as she did, often getting angry and taking that mood back to her family in the evening so they also felt the strain. After taking Impatiens for 2 months she was able to let go of her irritation and stress and neck/shoulder pains had also disappeared. This shows how our temperament affects our physical body also.

Flower remedies help us to become stronger

One lady came to me for a consultation saying how weak she felt, with no energy and pains in her legs. She described how she felt like a servant to her family, how they took her for granted, and how frightened she was of her son who bullied her. This person was obviously a Centaury type, so I prescribed this essence for her, along with Mimulus for her fears and also Oak. After one month she was feeling more energy, after another few months taking these remedies she was feeling stronger in herself and more able to stand up to her son, her fears dissolving. Gradually, as taking the essences her relationships around her changed for the better, with her family giving her more respect and no longer taking advantage of her. Our relationships are a direct reflection of us. As we change for the better, so do the people around us, for they have to start relating to us in a different way. When we no longer react, (or emotionally respond,) to the energies of others they can no longer draw us into their own drama's or personality imbalances and hence they have to change also. So, it is one of the biggest lessons for us to understand that we cannot change others only ourselves; but then our changes are reflected back to us. This is how we create our own reality, only by doing the inner work!

Flower remedies cleanse and purify us

One man had severe psoriasis on his feet for many years. Doctors and skin specialist gave many kinds of drugs and cream to clear it, all to no avail. The man decided he would try the flower remedies and after a consultation I could see that he carried feelings of guilt and lack of self-worth, along with the vague feeling that his feet were quite disgusting. I prescribed the remedies Crab Apple and Pine along with some others he needed 8 times per day. I also gave him large stock bottles of Crab Apple and Pine to put in all his baths (10 drops each). Altogether, he took these remedies quite sporadically for 6-8 months, as he often forgot to take them to work, but diligently continued to use them. At the end of this time the skin on his feet had healed up very considerably. I then prescribed Emergency Essence cream also to be rubbed on daily, as this is very healing and also contains Crab Apple and Pine. Our bodies are a direct reflection of our thought forms. As his mind and thoughts of himself were healed so too was his skin.

Flower remedies help us to be more intuitive and in touch with our inner guidance

One lady came to see me suffering from M.E.. Having been forced to leave a very stressful job after developing the illness – (a means of her spirit showing her a change was necessary!) this lady was learning the many lessons that this or any other illness provides us with to help us become clearer. When we realise that we only incarnate so that we may have many different earth plane experiences as a way of learning to overcome negativity and balance emotions, it is easier to learn and grow from each opportunity life offers.

As she took her appropriate essences she became much stronger but still did not feel she knew what her divine path was. Although she had learned to meditate, she was unable to distinguish between her ego and the true messages from her Spirit. I prescribed the remedies Wild Oat and Cerato and after taking these for one month, she came back to tell me that she knew very clearly where her path lay, and was much more positive as she was now following her inner guidance to learn something new which she was becoming very interested in. As we follow our own inner guidance and knowing, (which the ego or lower self of our nature can block with the negative patterns we have developed), so we blossom and heal. Flower essences help our spiritual growth.

Flower essences help us to let go and relax

One client was suffering greatly from muscular dystrophy, having been born severely physically handicapped and she had spent her life in a wheelchair. She was unable to move any part of her body except fingers, hands and head. Because of this severe condition, all her physical requirements were looked after by a team of care attendants. However, this lady had a very powerful mind and felt that she had to control her workers with her voice and she was continually calling out demands and needing to control her external circumstances. She was in much physical pain all the time. I prescribed the remedies Vine and Chicory which she took over a period of 9-12 months, during which time she was gradually feeling less physical pain as she let go of the need to control. Rigid thought forms cause tension in the physical body; as they are released so the body relaxes. As she learned how to let go of her control patterns, she became happier in herself and her pains were released. This lady was then able to enjoy her life in a far better way.

USING THE 38 ESSENCES

DIAGNOSIS AND PRESCRIPTION

Using these 38 flower essences is a very simple process as they work in a very natural, uncomplicated way. You do not (at the time of printing), require any particular qualifications to select essences for yourself or others. The reason for this is because flower essences are available to all, either from retail outlets or by post, as they are completely harmless to use, giving no side effects or contra-indications. There are two categories of essences, those which are needed to be taken over a longish time period to clear deep-rooted states and those needed in the moment.

EVERYDAY USE

Any of the flower essences can be taken to alleviate negative states in the moment. These can be extreme emotional states like the client needing Cherry Plum, to conditions like shock, sleeplessness, tiredness and feeling overwhelmed. Many of these patterns may just need a couple of doses of the essence to alleviate that state. Anyone in extreme pain will benefit from the correctly chosen essence, at that moment. This would be chosen according to the mood they are in at that time, (not always their usual nature!) Example – a person needing attention from those around when in difficulty, either physically or emotionally would need Chicory. Often as the chicory is taken they feel better and the discomfort goes.

If someone in severe pain is irritable and impatient for the pain to go, by them taking a few drops of Impatiens every 5 minutes, the pain goes as they become calmer.

If a person has a tendency to be the Agrimony type, they may keep the pain to themselves not wishing to upset others; then Agrimony would work in the same manner. The remedies are not a substitute for a medical doctor and are not intended to replace medical assistance. However, by giving the correct remedy(s) for that person they will very often be feeling better by the time the doctor arrives and the healing process will have been speeded up. In those acute cases always treat according to the mood or temperament the person is in at that time. The essences cannot be taken too often in these extreme states.

One mother phoned me up needing a diagnosis of essences for her baby. I knew that she had a set of these 38 in the house and "tuned-in" to the correct remedies. I was given the essences Holly and Impatiens through going within and hearing my inner voice. I told her this on the telephone and the diagnosis made complete sense when she then said he had a severe fever, high temperature and was screaming (anger and frustration). I then told her to give the baby the essences every 5 minutes and to also telephone her doctor. Within 2 hours she phoned back to say the fever he had all the previous night was now gone and his temperature dropped within 1 hour of taking the remedies, he was fine and the doctor was cancelled.

It was Edward Bach's vision that in the future each household would possess a set of the essences with someone in each family able to prescribe and diagnose them. These simple to use essences are such a valuable tool to have available in the home!

Some of the flower essences in this system are more obviously suited to assist in clearing transient states than others, although ANY of the 38 could be applicable to help someone in acute physical, emotional or mental distress in that moment. If one needs the vibrations of the plant now for energy, sudden mood changes, stress, panic, shock, etc., then take as follows:

EITHER: 2 drops direct from the stock bottle on tongue, ensuring the dropper does not touch the tongue as it could contaminate the contents with saliva. Repeat as necessary, every 10 minutes or half hour until the state has passed.

OR: 2 drops of stock in a small cup of tea or small glass of water/juice and sip slowly (4 drops in a mug). Repeat if necessary.

OLIVE – physical/mental tiredness – exhaustion.
HORNBEAM – mental tiredness – computer work – to wake up in the morning.
WHITE CHESTNUT – to stop thoughts going round in head – to sleep.
VERVAIN – for sleep and releasing tension.
ROCK ROSE – for panic attacks.
EMERGENCY ESSENCE – for panic attacks – shock – trauma – distressing news – for generally calming down – dentist or hospital visits – exams – driving tests – before and after operations.
CLEMATIS – for fainting – not feeling grounded – unconscious states, (rub on lips, pulse spots) or use Emergency essence.
ELM – feeling overwhelmed by ones responsibilities.
MUSTARD – for dispelling gloom.
CHERRY PLUM – PMT – irrational states – fears of losing control.
IMPATIENS – pain – frustration – impatience.

ANY of the other 38 essences can be taken in the same way – to clear extreme negative states – not just those listed above; these are just some of the more common passing states.

These essences may also be needed over a period of several weeks or months, once the initial extreme state has cleared, 6 or 8 times a day to fully clear the imbalance, thus ensuring it does not return.

TO CLEAR DEEP ROOTED STATES OF MIND.

Essences need to be taken over a longer time period

We all need to clear blockages which keep us away from feeling whole, balanced and happy (our true state). These blockages will also eventually cause physical pain or illness if we do not work at clearing them away. The blocks themselves may be emotional imbalances or negative mental patterns. We have all carried both from before birth and after. Our soul chooses for us the exact moment of birth, knowing exactly which aspects of personality we need to develop, balance or utilise on our chosen path. This is because our soul carries the memory of all aspects of personalities, deeds and achievements from previous incarnations. There is a spiritual cycle of initiations we each have to undertake on our earth plane path. For instance, someone choosing to balance fire energy in this life would be born with as many planets as possible placed in fire at the time of birth. It is not as simple as saying the Sun sign is Aries or Leo; this would be just one planet. An accurate astrological (natal) chart can be drawn up to see the balance of earth, air, fire and water, also the masculine and feminine energies needing balance. Too much fire energy creates impatience, jealousy, anger, fanaticism, or domineering attitudes, etc. To bring balance to these patterns you could take the essences, Impatiens, Holly, Vervain or Vine. To bring your personality to balance would bring you patience, inner peace and stillness. Thus you would be healing and developing qualities to help you and your soul's growth. Any of these unbalanced fire states can cause much physical tension, high blood pressure, varicose veins, headaches, etc. It is equally so for any of the other energetic frequencies within our make-up from birth, i.e. water, earth, air, each having their own patterns and eventual accompanying physical symptoms if left unhealed. In addition to this personality we choose before birth, we also "take on board" the personality traits of our parents, nanny or those having most influence on us in childhood. These traits can be positive or negative. For instance, my own birth chart shows no trace of impatience or planets in Aries and yet I needed to take the essence Impatiens on and off for a few years to bring total balance to that aspect of my personality. It was very extreme and caused me much difficulty and tension. Where did it come from?? My mother's side of the family carried the trait very severely, so in childhood one of the impressions I took in was that it was natural to be very quick and impatient and in this extreme state. By looking at ourselves, inwardly and honestly, we can see our own imbalances and which remedies we need. Then look to your parents, remember scenes from childhood, ask you higher self to show you in meditation* or the dream state the patterns from them that have most influenced you. This will also indicate to you the remedies you need. If there was extreme distress, sadness or fear, you need to practise

*My meditation CD "Healing the Inner Child" is a wonderful tool for this purpose.

sending your parents, or those responsible, love and forgiveness. Remember, they may have developed their own anger, fear, etc. in childhood as they too are here to learn to overcome difficulties and grow. We each act from the consciousness we have in any given moment. As we change and our consciousness raises we may choose to act in a different way, a more loving way. That does not make what we did in the past "bad" and we do not need to feel guilty, it simply was a learning process. As we take the appropriate essences we are more able to send love and forgiveness to others and also to ourselves. This helps us to heal and become whole. The essences used in this way, over a period of time, be it months or years, may be looked upon as that most powerful tool, PREVENTATIVE MEDICINE. By treating our personality, even though our physical vehicle (body) may appear to be fit and healthy at present, we are helping to keep illness and disease at bay. Indeed, the clearer we become, the more illness appears to become a thing of the past – a memory of how we used to be. This is certainly so for the more minor ailments such as colds, viruses, aches, pains, headaches, PMT and menopausal symptoms. Case histories show that this process also works equally well on dis-ease depending on the lessons and growth pattern the soul has chosen karmically in this life.

One of the most wonderful aspects of working on our lower personality (or ego states) in this way is that as our positive qualities grow so our higher self can bring through and manifest our more spiritual qualities. Therefore, the gradual change in our lower self brings the ability to find it easier to meditate, be at peace, hear our intuition and inner guidance, develop love and forgiveness and reflect the radiance of our spirit through our personality. Hence comes the desire to become a channel for healing energies to help others (see my book on Eternal Light® Healing Energies.) The ancient caveat is AS ABOVE SO BELOW! This is how we are meant to be! This is our divine inheritance, we all carry light within us.

To work in this deeper way, you may choose up to 7 (maximum) flower essences and mix them together. Yes, our mind can assimilate and work on many different states at any one time. Originally, when the essences were first developed a maximum of 6 was advised. However, things change, nothing is static. Dr. Bach states now, (from the other dimensions) that our consciousness has risen so much since the 1930's, space travel, mass media, women's lib. etc., that our minds are now capable of working on more aspects at once. However, often it feels more appropriate to just focus on 2 or 3 aspects you wish to change, it is then easier to watch the changes. The 38 flower essences in this system, bought from Heartsong are all stock potency. That means they can be diluted. So they become a very economical way of natural treatment. To make what is termed a dosage bottle, i.e. an individual treatment bottle of up to 7 essences, take a clean, empty, amber glass dropper bottle (size, up to 30 ml) and add just 2 drops of each chosen essence. Then add a teaspoon of brandy, any other spirit, or cider vinegar as a preservative, then top up the bottle with still spa or bottled water. If this is not obtainable then tap water must be boiled. Shake, label, and take 4 drops on the tongue at least 4 times a day, 10 minutes or more away from food or on an empty stomach. If the states are deep-rooted it would be wise to take the mixture 8 times a day or more for adults, for children 4 times is often enough. This will speed up the process. The more frequently the mixture is taken the sooner the difficulties will be alleviated. Remember, this system of essences work very gently and you cannot overdose or become addicted. You may also take drops from the stock level bottle in the same way. Guidance is that this can be 20% more effective.

IMPORTANT

You cannot overdose with the 38 essences. Adult dose 4-8 times a day or more. A child may only need 3-4 times a day, except in acute states when any essence or combination may be taken every 5-10 minutes. The essences cannot interfere with any other form of treatment or medicine, except to speed up the healing process, and are complementary medicine at its best.

Likewise, the essences cannot be cancelled out by or interfere with any other medicine, be it allopathic (drugs), herbal, ayurvedic, etc. The essences may be taken alongside any other treatment. You cannot become addicted to the essences. If they are diluted as above, in a dosage bottle, the brandy or preservative can hardly be tasted. If you do not wish to taste any brandy, or are allergic to it, you may make up a dosage bottle with only the water. Keep it in the fridge between doses so that it does not go off. The essences may be used by all of any age, babies, children, adults and the elderly all benefit from the essences. In pregnancy, the essences will be helping the baby as well as the mother and during childbirth, the Emergency combination is wonderful. Many midwives are now using this to ease the pain and trauma their patients are in.

Animals, birds and plants all benefit from the essences. Indeed, babies and animals are very open to any kind of healing energy and respond very quickly. They are not preconditioned into thinking, "how can this work?" Always take essences away from food if possible to get best results. 10 minutes or more before/after food or on an empty stomach is best.

Taking the "wrong" essence can do no harm at all. If it is not needed or has already worked it will be benign and cancel itself out. No harm can be done. If you do not wish to make up a dosage bottle, you may put 2 drops from the stock bottle of each chosen essence into a small glass or cup of water, fruit juice or any drink, except coffee, (a mug would be 4 drops) and sip as often as needed. This is good for acute or passing states and clears the imbalance quickly. For long term treatment a dosage bottle is more economical and you are more likely to remember it if carried around. As you take the essence it can be helpful to keep a diary or a note of how you are feeling, day-to-day or weekly. This will help you to see any changes taking place. When you feel that an essence has worked leave it out the next time you make up a dosage bottle and continue with the rest in the combination. If you feel a different state has come up for treatment you may then add the appropriate essence to the existing bottle. Our healing process is rather like unpeeling the layers of an onion. As aspects of personality on the surface are cleared away with essence use, often one finds suppressed or deep rooted patterns coming to the surface for treatment to be transmuted. Often these are aspects one previously had no conscious knowledge of. Gradually, as we continue to work with this process, we become clearer, happier and more attuned to God Consciousness, the Universal Mind or the Supreme Creative Force through our Higher-Self as our consciousness rises.

AFFIRMATIONS – by affirming the positive aspects within ourselves, each time we take a dose, we are potentising the essence even more. The positive aspects are all within us already, our true self. They simply become hidden by the negative aspects of our personality. The essence of each plant contains the positive qualities contained within us; so, as they are taken they trigger our inner Divine nature and reveal to us our true self. I can remember Dr. Edward Bach likening the healing qualities of the essences to the sun, melting away the snow on the mountains. You may make your own affirmations as long as they are positive and in the NOW.

> i.e. for Mimulus – "I am filled with courage."
> (NOT, I will feel more courage)

PRESCRIBING ESSENCES FOR OTHERS

When seeking to help others, try not to be pushy or over-enthusiastic, (Vervain!), this will often have the opposite effect and be very off-putting. Usually it is a more natural process. As you obtain a set of essences and start working on yourself, friends and family observe your transformation and approach you for a combination for themselves. Let them know that you have the set and are happy to prepare them for anyone. If you have children or animals try working on those first. As you start to see positive results your confidence will grow. It is not difficult to learn about the 38 essences. Start by getting to know the ones you need and are working with. Look around at friends, family, TV characters and try to see which essences they need. Do they need to release anxiety and fears? Are they critical and judgmental of others? Do they put on a brave face and bottle things up?

As well as left brain rational knowledge, there are other ways of choosing the correct essences. These are right-brained, or intuitive techniques which are often the more accurate. A good flower essence practitioner will usually be working in a balanced way with knowledge gained plus their intuitive abilities.

Often a person's difficulties are not always apparent even after a discussion or consultation. They may wish to hide certain facts from you which would help you to select the essences needed. This is done, sometimes subconsciously, through fear, pride, or guilt feelings. Ask the person to be as open with you as possible and reassure them that the conversation is strictly private. You will also learn lessons in integrity. You may ask them how they wish to be helped at present. Other leading questions are, "how was your childhood?, did any trauma's occur that you remember?, how do you feel now about that? What is your relationship like with your husband/wife/ partner? What qualities would you like to develop?

Develop your listening abilities; let them talk about themselves, and watch. Much will be revealed by the personality in their mannerisms and body language. Even over the telephone impressions can be picked up. Are they hesitant, nervous, over talkative? Do they speak quickly or slowly? Do they have a stutter or stammer? A person needing Impatiens will walk very quickly up your path, if the door is not opened immediately they will knock again, impatiently. Someone needing Scleranthus will be unable to decide between dates for an appointment. They may sound doubtful that the essences can help them, Gentian. They may sound resentful about paying, Willow. As you observe people you will soon start to see what essence is needed.

The nice thing about this work is that you do not need qualifications, only a genuine desire to help yourself and others to heal. A tool for the layperson – who often goes on to become a practitioner in their own right by seeing clients on a fee-paying basis. Then it is important that the client values the essences and time you spend with them, your knowledge, etc., by paying in monetary terms. If you have a lack of self worth, or lack confidence, try to encourage others to value you and your work. You can also take Pine or Larch! Everyone can give something, however small, towards your time and costs. You will have to buy bottles, and stocks as they run out, labels, water and brandy. Although these costs are minimal they need to be covered. It often takes an hour for a proper consultation, to explain what the essences are, how they work and to mix your client's combination bottles. They will need 2 x 30ml. bottles (which you can purchase at most chemists) to last them 3-4 weeks, at a dosage rate of 6-8 times a day, more for longer. It is important to sterilise dosage bottles being returned from others. Take apart the glass dropper, rubber and plastic top and together with glass bottle, place all in a clean saucepan used only for this purpose (not aluminium). Cover with water and bring to boil, turn down heat and simmer for 10 minutes. Dry with a clean cloth or leave to drain, covered, before re-assembling. Never use detergents or washing up liquids etc.

If you do the work of helping your fellow man/woman to be healed full time or even part time you deserve to live and earn an income from it! Dr. Edward Bach found that when he tried to give essences away very few wanted them. When he charged a small amount the interest grew. If someone really has no money, some other energy exchange can take place. Maybe they can perform a small service for you, baby-sit, clean your home, cook you meal etc. Money is only God's energy – a form of exchange. This is often forgotten in today's society.

WAYS TO DEVELOP INTUITIVE DIAGNOSIS

DOWSING

Try learning to dowse for essences with a pendulum. This is easy to do and if you work from a centred space, still, and without your ego involved, your subconscious mind can bring through accurate essences your conscious mind had not thought of. To be sure you are doing this unconditionally, always ask for the Highest Divine will to come through, try to step back and have no attachment to the outcome, then your personality will not influence the pendulum. There are many books on dowsing available. Do be aware, though, that dowsing is only a step towards contacting your intuition or higher self and will need to be released as you further develop your inner guidance. When I first started this work, many years ago, I started dowsing to double check what my intuition and inner voice were telling me. I was told by the Ascended Master guiding me that I had to trust what I got but the temptation to get the pendulum out when I was uncertain was too tempting. What happened? I put it down in front of me one day and it disappeared completely. I bought another and when I got it out to use it, in front of a client a few weeks later it was snatched out of my hand with great force by an invisible hand and smashed on the floor in front of me.

I got the message! Both myself and my client saw Victor Bullen standing over me with a smile on his face.

DEVELOPING INTUITION

Try meditating with the thought of the other person (or yourself) in your mind and ask to be given any essences needed. With practise you may find yourself having an idea, or getting words of essences (this is clairaudience) or pictures of the flowers (this is clairvoyance). If it doesn't come immediately, sleep on it, asking for it to come through in your dreams. Remember these are usually symbolic and you may need to translate! You can develop sensitivity by running the palms of your hands or fingers over the top of each row of essences in an open box, or try in their aura an inch or so above. You may feel a "pull", or an energy, tingling or vibration over the essence needed.

As you are talking, listening to, or even just thinking of a person, an essence will drop into your head. Trust this guidance, even if it is not obviously suitable, give it anyway. No harm can come from giving a "wrong" essence, it will be benign and will simply cancel itself out. It may be the very catalyst needed, especially if someone has taken remedies for a while and feels stuck. (see CATALYSTS, further down).

PHOTOGRAPHIC DIAGNOSIS

Use the photographs in this book as a diagnostic tool. Subconsciously, we know exactly which plant essence we need, we are drawn to it. Ask a person what is their favourite flower or tree and see if it is one of the 38. This way they are more involved in their own healing process. Another method is to close your eyes and centre yourself, asking in your mind to be shown the right one for you, either for now or longer term, and then let the book fall open at the right page. Meditate by looking at the picture, then if it feels right take the essence. Using my Bach flower cards as a divination tool is another powerful way and very self empowering for others to choose their own essences.

THE CATALYSTS

If unsure which essences are needed or there seems to be too many required, try using the catalyst essences. These are Star of Bethlehem, Holly and Wild Oat. Star of Bethlehem may be the one if they have had some trauma in the past which could be blocking them. Those needing Holly will usually have a ruddy complexion, they can be very hot people. Wild Oat is for the cooler, paler types. Often, taking one or more of these helps to make the picture clearer after a few weeks. They can also be very useful if someone seems stuck after taking the essences for a while.

HOW TO TREAT BABIES AND ANIMALS

BABIES

Unlike adults and children, babies cannot tell you how they are feeling in words. Therefore it becomes even more important to develop intuitive diagnosis. Again, there will be body language and it is very easy to spot a baby that needs Mimulus; he or she will be nervous and uncomfortable with sudden noises and bright lights. A baby needing lots of unnecessary attention needs Chicory, one that is unable to tell its mother that it is nappy changing time may need Agrimony and so on.

Drops may be mixed in a baby's bottle, but no more than 2 or 3 essences together. If being breast fed drops can be rubbed on the mothers nipples at each feeding time.

I was recently called to give healing to a friend's baby in the intensive care unit, in hospital. This baby had a difficult birth, could not be fed and was on a drip. Several times during the healing I was guided to put drops of Emergency Essence on her lips, Brow chakra and solar plexus. Other points could also be pulse spots in this situation or if unconscious. She reacted very positively each time. Being in a critical condition for months, after much healing and essences she is now home and very well.

ANIMALS

Cats and dogs dosage, 6-8 drops of each essence in a small bowl of water or milk. Some will also take drops on their tongues or from your palm.

Although an animal may need any or many of the 38 essences, sometimes there are characteristics peculiar to that species. Cats for instance, often need Water Violet, like the upright, proud, Egyptian type cat (this type can develop arthritis or rheumatism). Or if nervous, Aspen, Mimulus or Rock Rose. Psychic cats, who see energies in the room when you can see none may need Walnut to give them protection or Cherry Plum if they "start." Often they are seeing angels, or guides on the other dimensions or simply waves of energy.

Dogs also have their own characteristics, which again could be any of the 38. "One man" dogs like German Shepherds often need Chicory as they can become too possessive of their owners or even Holly if they want to bite anyone else sparring for attention. One dog I treated, a Labrador, was given the essence Beech as he seemed quite intolerant. Gradually, the arthritis in his back legs and joints improved. Rigidity of the mind reflected in the body. Another dog, a poodle with arthritis so severe he could not climb the stairs in the owners house was bounding up them after a course of the appropriate essences. My own dog, Heidi, was a rescued one and needed lots of Cherry Plum and Vervain and she was quite "over the top," unbalanced and over-enthusiastic. After a course of treatment it was as though a light had been switched on in her brain and she was changed beyond belief. Heidi has now gone into transition, she died overnight with no symptoms of illness beforehand, and very quickly and easily. She chose the very time when my work was about to take me abroad a lot with much travelling and even with help, it would have been quite difficult for me to provide a loving, caring home for her. She was not happy in kennels and was a good age, 13 years. I was of course, very distressed by her passing, as she had been my great friend and protector for many years, but the essences helped me to come to terms with my bereavement very quickly. Star of Bethlehem, Walnut and Honeysuckle were all good choices at that time. It helped that I was able to tune into her on other levels and her spirit visited the house until I had got over her passing. Often I would look up and see her in her favourite chair. I communicated with her and she told me that her life's purpose had been fulfilled. She had been "sent" to me to open me up to my Divine purpose – without the need to give her flower essences I would not have seen their wonderful healing effects. This led me to think, if they can help animals in this way, how well they must help humans and I soon started working as a practitioner with a deep feeling of satisfaction in serving mankind and watching them heal.

BIRDS

Birds are very fragile. Often a cat will catch one and bring it into the house without actually harming it. Taking it from the mouth gently, you will feel the poor bird is frozen in terror. However, a few drops of Emergency essence dropped in and around its beak may soon have it flying out the door, if it has not been injured. Essences may be put in the water of caged birds. Birds with skin problems would benefit from Crab Apply and if scratching a lot, may need Impatiens or Holly also for the irritation, there are many other possibilities. When seeing caged birds I often tune into their sadness and gloom at their lack of freedom, Gentian, Gorse, Mustard or Sweet Chestnut are all appropriate essences to help them become happier in their unnatural environment.

LARGER ANIMALS

As with humans the golden rule is still to treat the individual according to their moods, or characteristics. Therefore each horse, cow or goat will need a different essence or combination. One way for farmers to breed happy and healthy animals is to treat his livestock with flower essences. You can make combinations in the same way as for humans but larger animals will need larger doses. Horses for instance would need around 20 drops of each chosen stock essence in a bucket of water.

Each time they had a drink they would also receive the healing energies. One horse I treated was quite highly strung and often refused a certain jump. I gave Vervain and Mimulus in large stock bottles to be put in his water daily and after 2 months the horse was fine, much better and a problem on his hind leg had healed. I had also given him some hands on healing.

Emergency Essence is a great help at calming an animal down before an event. Show dogs or cats will be much calmer if given before and during travelling to the show and just before going on. The same for horses be they show jumpers or race horses. Their performance will be so much better if they are not nervous or in trauma beforehand. I used Emergency essence once on a cow which had just given birth a few days before. The calf was very weak and unable to stand up as the cow had developed mastitis and was so sore she was unable to feed her calf . I asked the farmer if I could give some essences to them, he had nothing to lose. He loved his animals and the drugs given by the vet had not helped. With his help I put lots of Emergency Essence on both animals tongues. While waiting for this to take effect, I rubbed in Emergency Essence cream on the cow's udders as they were too sore to put the liquid drops on. It was very hot and after half an hour I again gave them more doses and quickly the cow went to her water to drink for the first time that day. The calf then started trying to get up and with our help she got on her legs and also started drinking. I added more Emergency Essence to the water with some Oak and Olive to give them energy. Both animals needed no further help apart from more udder cream. Just one example of how animals can be helped through any illness or difficulty. This is not a substitute for veterinary assistance, simply extra, natural help.

I was once invited to give a talk on the flower essences to a goat club. I agreed to do it as although I had never treated a goat, the same rules apply for all animals. It appeared from the audience that most of their animals were wayward creatures, very headstrong and bullying, although there were one or two exceptions of course. It would therefore appear to be Vine and Holly as the main goat characteristics with a bit of Chestnut Bud thrown in for good measure as many said their goats did not appear to learn their lessons. As usual, each goat would be treated as an individual with its own personal essences. They say that pets take on the personality of their owners, maybe the audience also needed those essences. Our pets, often, are therefore simply mirror reflections to show us what we need to work on ourselves. I have certainly found this with my animals.

THE SEVEN GROUPS & KARMIC FLOWER REMEDIES

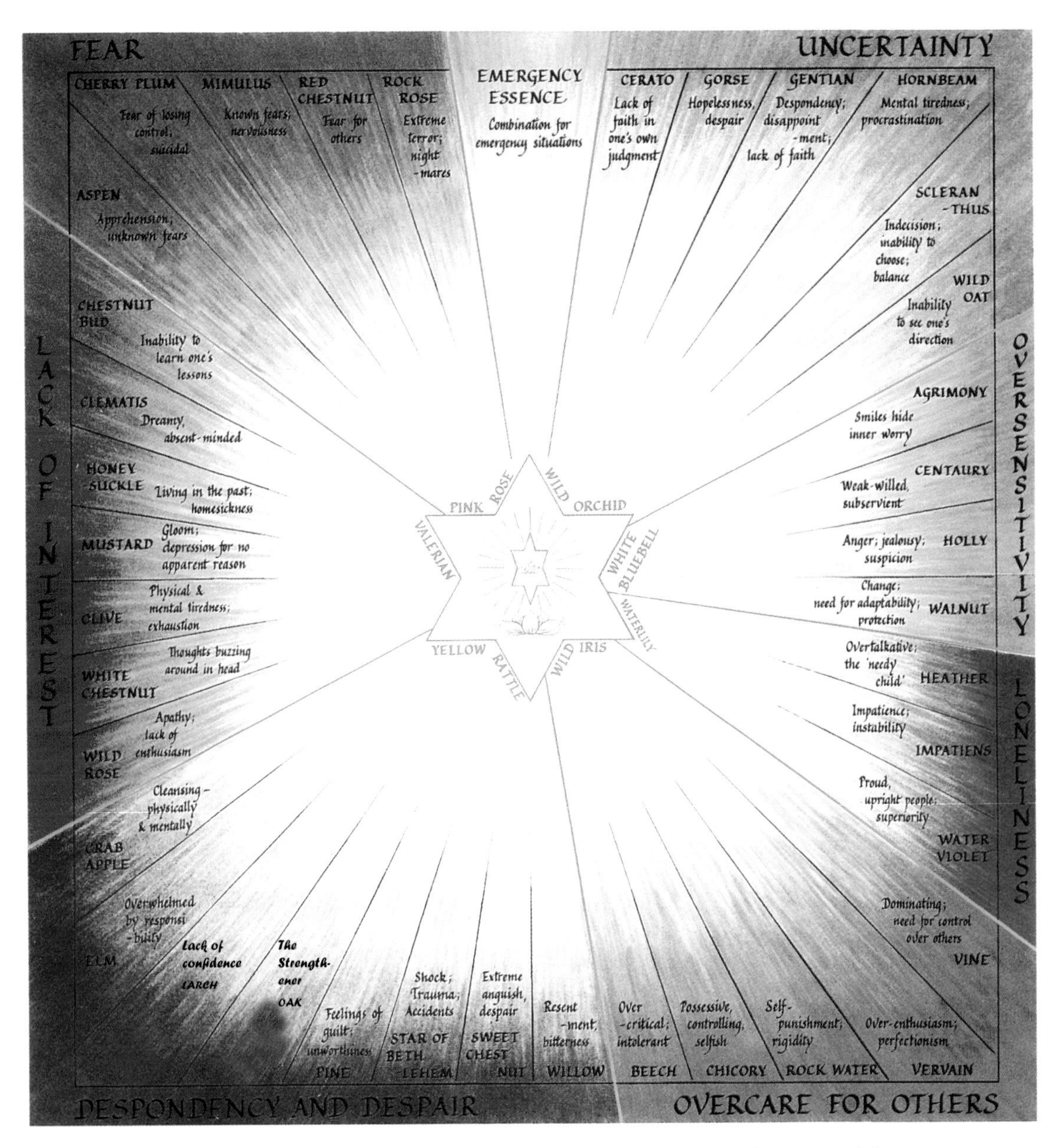

38 traditional Essences round the border; 7 Karmic Essences for deeper-rooted states round the Star. The Essence needs to be taken when in the inharmonious state described. These liquid energies release into the Light for transmutation all that is not love. The negative states are transmuted into Higher Consciousness as symbolised by the Six-pointed Star.

THE 12 HEALERS AND SEVEN GROUPS

Dr. Edward Bach named the first twelve flower essences that he discovered, "the Twelve Healers." Through observing the nature and personality types of his patients he had noted that some were very distinctive. These he likened to the "constitutional" types found in homeopathy, although with flower essences it is only the mental and emotional states of personality we are observing, nothing else. These 12 essences then are very important in the understanding of this natural system and indeed, humankind. If you look to yourself, your family and friends you will see the truth of these aids. Most people will fall into one particular type, others will be a combination of 2 or 3 of these 12. As with all remedies you do not need to treat when someone is in the positive state, only when this becomes unbalanced and is in the negative state. The states can be likened to a see-saw; the polarities at either end and in the middle the balance point. Most people will usually need at least one of the 12 healers (along with any of the other essences in combination), on a regular basis, over a minimum of 3 months to bring them closer to their balance point. By working in this way, you can make massive leaps forward in change, transformation and soul growth. Often it may be necessary to take it for 6 months or more until the positive aspects are observed and felt at all times. This may be needed between 6-8 times a day from a dosage bottle and can be mixed with any of the other essences in this set. The others may not be needed for such long periods, although some of the other states can also become very deep rooted. Let me give you some examples:

A person with a mainly MIMULUS disposition, nervous, quiet, with some known fears; may also need perhaps Larch for self-confidence, or Agrimony to help speak up or Centaury to give inner strength (or any of the other essences).

A character with an unbalanced VINE personality will be very strong willed, rigid, and dominant but may also be proud and aloof, (Water Violet) or impatient (Impatiens). Thus he would need a mixture of all three.

The 12 healers may also be likened to certain Astrological types which I have given here. There are also several others which could be ascribed to the 12 zodiac signs, although they may not be one of the 12 healers. It is not always as obvious as, say, being a Libra Sun sign and needing Scleranthus, but it may be used as a guide. (See recommended reading for Peter Damian's Astrological Study)

THE TWELVE ASTROLOGICAL SIGNS

SIGN	ESSENCE	OTHERS POSSIBLE
Aries	Impatiens	Vine
Taurus	Gentian	Holly
Gemini	Cerato	Wild Oat
Cancer	Clematis	Red Chestnut, Chicory
Leo	Vervain	Vine
Virgo	Centaury	Beech
Libra	Scleranthus	Hornbeam
Scorpio	Chicory	Cherry Plum
Sagittarius	Agrimony	Holly
Capricorn	Mimulus	Larch
Aquarius	Water Violet	
Pisces	Rock Rose	Walnut

To help you see how this system of diagnosis works, let me state my own case.

The first natal chart I had drawn up by an astrologer was inaccurate. Why? Because I found out later that the chart needs to be at EXACTLY the time of birth. If it is out by 30 minutes that would make a difference of at least six degrees. If hours out then obviously, a much greater difference giving the chart and interpretation another meaning. My first chart which was drawn up many years ago, I did not dowse, or ask my spirit for the exact birth time as I was unable to do so at that time, neither did the astrologer. When a later one was drawn up for me and I was given the reading, it made much more sense. From the final chart I got 3 planets in Leo (I have often needed to take Vervain), 3 planets in Scorpio (Chicory has been one of my most needed long term essences) and Sun in Libra. Again I had taken much Scleranthus and putting together these essences with the impatience I picked up in childhood, (Impatiens) and the need for Agrimony, another family trait, and my often needed Oak, this would have been an excellent combination bottle for me. Now I very rarely need any of these essences, I have now taken enough to bring my personality into balance.

If I occasionally get out of balance I know immediately and am able to change it with my thoughts because the pattern is simply on the surface now (not deep rooted or subconscious) and much easier to see and let go of. A few drops of the essence would also do the job.

THE SEVEN MAIN GROUPS

Edward Bach placed the essences into 7 different groups, depending on the aspects they were treating. These groups are listed below.

FEAR
Cherry Plum
Rock Rose
Red Chestnut
Aspen
Mimulus

LONELINESS
Impatiens
Water Violet
Heather

OVERSENSITIVITY
Agrimony
Centaury
Holly
Walnut

DESPAIR & DESPONDENCY
Pine
Larch
Star of Bethlehem
Willow
Sweet Chestnut
Crab Apple
Elm
Oak

LACK OF INTEREST IN PRESENT CIRCUMSTANCES
Clematis
Honeysuckle
Chestnut Bud
Olive
Mustard
White Chestnut
Wild Rose

INDECISION / UNCERTAINTY
Scleranthus
Cerato
Gentian
Gorse
Hornbeam
Wild Oat

OVERCARE & CONCERN FOR OTHERS
Beech
Vine
Vervain
Chicory
Rock Water

Agrimony *Agrimonia Eupatoria*

AGRIMONY

POSITIVE QUALITIES

- Helps to open and clear throat chakra.
- The ability to speak out freely without worrying what others are thinking or how it affects them.
- Speaking Divine Truth from the heart.
- Not needing others to like you.
- The ability to be ones' true self.
- Does not need to entertain others.
- Inner fulfilment without the need for outside stimulation.
- A true Peacemaker.

NEGATIVE STATE

- Hiding inner worries behind a smile and a joke.
- Laughs and giggles instead of true words (listen to an Agrimony type on the telephone).
- Seeking satisfaction/fulfilment in addictive behaviour and substances. i.e. alcohol, drugs, smoking, sex, food.
- Inner restlessness and lots of outer movements, need for travelling and excitement
- Restless sleep patterns.
- Unable to express ones needs and emotions.
- Throat chakra blocked or closed.
- Needs to keep the peace at all costs to self.
- Inner turmoil kept to one's self.

The main trait of the Agrimony type is the need to keep the peace at all costs. They dislike enormously upsetting others as they are afraid of emotional outbursts, being unable/afraid to express their own emotions. They will go to great lengths not to rock the boat in all circumstances and this particularly takes its toll on them physically, emotionally and in their relationships. They are constantly being misunderstood as they do not speak out and others often have to mind-read or assume what the Agrimony type is thinking or feeling. Because of these difficulties the personality type often tries to loose itself in addictions, hoping to find the true inner peace it so desperately seeks in a bottle, or through drug taking, smoking, etc. Agrimony types worry excessively, internally, but are unable to express their concerns. When asked how they feel, they say "I'm fine", even if their world is falling apart.

Anyone with BLOCKED EMOTIONS needs Agrimony! This is usually a more long-term flower essence as this negative trait is usually very deep rooted. It can stem from childhood where the personality has been suppressed, often by a parent who will not allow the child to express itself in a proper way. One example of this is the parent who teaches the child it is wrong to cry or express emotion, usually because the parent themselves is unable to do so or had similar parents. "Children must be seen and not heard" is another Victorian quote which has been passed down to future generations. Children must be encouraged to express their needs and emotions, to cry as well as laugh and to bring through their creative expression, through colours, music, etc. The throat chakra is the point for creative and true expression to take place. When this chakra is blocked, or in extreme cases closed down, the creative force which moves up from the sacral area and chakra is unable to be expressed and can then create physical problems. Continual sore throats, swollen glands, tonsillitis, voice loss and thyroid problems are all due to the throat chakra not functioning fully. If this happens in a young child then it is a good sign that the child has incarnated into this life with a closed or blocked throat chakra due to difficulties in previous lifetimes. Either suppression of speaking or speaking ones' truths and being persecuted for it, can be causes of the spirit choosing a physical vehicle with a throat chakra problem. This is all of course subconscious, but often regression or meditation will reveal these lives. As the Agrimony is taken so one is able to clear these blockages.

If you have been this type from childhood be prepared to take the essence for 6 months or more, 6 or 8 times a day for an adult. Gradually, you will see wonderful changes. Also the Throat chakra combination remedy will assist this process.

ASPEN

POSITIVE QUALITIES

- The ability to go to new situations and places with ease and calmness.
- To be unafraid of the unknown.
- To be totally at ease with other dimensions, i.e. spiritual and astral levels.
- Calm and balanced when experiencing or hearing of psychic phenomena, spirit world, ghosts, etc.
- Able to meditate or go to sleep without fear.
- Able to adapt easily and fearlessly to different energies, i.e. lay-lines, earth vortexes, sacred sites, etc.

Aspen *Populus Tremula*

NEGATIVE STATES

- Creepy, unknown fears.
- Anxiety with no logical explanation for it.
- Feeling of "goose-bumps" or that someone walked over your grave.
- Apprehension without knowing why.
- Great feelings of coldness and sudden pale expression.
- Sudden shivers, shaking or trembling without explanation.
- Children needing the light on at night.
- Fears of darkness and death, nightmares (see also Rock Rose).
- Very open and oversensitive to lower astral plane energies.

The flower essence Aspen is made from the catkins of the delicate but strong tree. When viewed in a breeze the leaves of the Aspen tremble, very much like the person needing the remedy. When the personality is in the negative Aspen state there is a lack of contact at personality level with the higher self. Therefore there is the inability to sense or feel at one with other dimensions, particularly the 4th dimension. The fourth dimension is frequented by many "lost souls" or discarnate spirits. Beings who having transited from this life have remained stuck on the astral levels for various reasons. Often, because of negativity in the personality before passing over, the spirit decides not to go to the light or higher dimensions to continue learning and growing but chooses (we still have free will at this stage) to remain close to the earth. Often this is to stay close to loved ones, although often this "unseen" presence contributes to the negative Aspen state in those they profess to love. Other times the spirit chooses to remain because there is an inability to let go of possessions, relationships, houses, or even the experiences of earthly tastes, especially those personalities with addictions. They choose to stay, and often will try to relive addictions through an incarnate personality with similar tastes. Hence alcoholics and drug addicts attract these energies to them and the energies can penetrate through their weakened auric field, often at the Solar Plexus, Base or Throat chakras. As one takes the flower essence Aspen, so one looses the fears and apprehensive feelings associated with the subtle energies of the astral and other realms of being. As the higher self floods the conscious mind with courage and releases the fears, so an auric cloak is built up around the subtle bodies through which those energies will find it much more difficult to penetrate. When in the balanced Aspen state one is able to feel, sense or experience other dimensional frequencies without fear. Often the best mediums and channels for higher energies are those who have expressed these fears and transmuted them.

Beech *Fagus Sylvatica*

BEECH

POSITIVE QUALITIES

- Tolerant of others, beliefs, creeds, colour, race, etc.
- Unaffected by the habits of others.
- At peace with oneself and the universe.
- Non judgmental, flexible.
- Does not judge oneself, loving all aspects of one's character.
- Allows others to go about their work without the need to criticise or judge.

NEGATIVE STATES

- Very critical of self and others.
- Judgmental of others and situations (a reflection of own judgement against self projected out).
- Can be racist or intolerant of different creeds, cultures and beliefs; often upholds class structures.
- Rigid and judgmental towards themselves – this rigidity of thought often creates rigidity of the body.
- Easily irritated by habits, gestures of others.
- Narrow minded, intolerant, arrogant.

When a person is critical and judgmental of others it is simply a reflection of their own rigid attitude to themselves. This negative pattern can, however, make life very difficult for those around them. They perceive that their criticism is for the good of others but it simply does not allow others the freedom to be themselves. The people around them then become defensive and afraid of doing anything for fear of criticism. Often this pattern may come from childhood when a parent or teacher may have been judging everything they did. A young child will then take this pattern on board as their own, thinking this is a normal way to behave, knowing no other. They then become critical of themselves and all that they do. As the Beech remedy is taken so they can learn to love themselves and know that they and others are only doing their best, as they know how, according to their level of consciousness. As their attitude changes so does their physical body as it becomes more supple and less rigid. Stiffness of joints such as arthritis is one of the physical reactions I have seen related to a critical attitude to life. Often it is possible to diagnose this essence when a person admits to becoming irritated by the habits of others around them, often, seemingly silly little things like the way someone eats, taps their feet or coughs. With a negative Beech personality in the house, leaving the top off the toothpaste tube can become a full scale war if one is not careful. Beech flower essence is working on the heart chakra, to help the individual love themselves and others unconditionally.

Centaury *Centaurium Erythraea*

CENTAURY

POSITIVE QUALITIES

- Able to serve without becoming subservient or a slave.
- Can say "No" when necessary, without feeling bad about it.
- Respect for oneself and one's own time and space.
- To be able to value oneself without needing to feel needed.
- To allow others to love you for yourself and not for what you do for them.
- To honour the need for spiritual service in whatever form it takes, joyfully.
- Strength of purpose and will power.

NEGATIVE STATES

- Unable to say "No" to others.
- Puts needs of others before own needs.
- Subservient personality, a doormat type.
- Personality not allowed to form.
- Creativity blocked.
- Overworked, becomes tired, worn-out and ill.
- Physically weak.
- Lacking in will power.

Being subservient is not the same thing as being in Divine Service. The latter is our true path in life, serving Mother/Father God, Divine Intelligence, our own spirit in a dedicated way through service to others. The service that is our Divine path may be through any occupation or relationship, be it road-sweeper or doctor, nanny or mother of a family. It is the work we chose to come and do before incarnating to learn and grow through helping others. In this we will find joy and will be able to honour ourselves during this process. The time that Centaury is needed is when, through a weak will, we allow others who are more dominant than ourselves to control us. We allow them to sap our energy and destroy our personality, thus our development and our inner growth becomes stunted. As Centaury is taken so we become inwardly stronger and our own will becomes more evident. We all need will power to be able to do things in the world or achieve our purpose. Gradually, we are more able to stand up for ourselves and say "no" when necessary. It is vital that we are able to do this; otherwise the more dominant Vine type personalities will totally dominate us if we allow them to. Thus we take back our own power, then we really start growing spiritually and at personality level. What happens when one is in the negative Centaury state is that our energy becomes sapped and drained, often you can see this type in service to others, as a carer, assistant in nursing home, someone who have given up a career and life to look after an elderly relative to the extreme, not looking after their own needs and never having a day off, often with no outside life at all. Often, they will have virtually no vitality and clairvoyantly I can see no red or orange in their aura, the will coming from the base chakra and the creative energy from the sacral chakra. As they become stronger and learn to love themselves through taking Centaury they become their true self and these colours return to their aura.

Cerato *Ceratostigma Willmottiana*

CERATO

POSITIVE QUALITIES

- Trust in ones' inner guidance/knowing.
- Allowing oneself to follow that guidance.
- Decisive.
- Inner communication with Higher Self.
- Getting the right answers in all situations.
- More dream recall.

NEGATIVE STATES

- Indecisive, unable to choose when faced with many possibilities (see also Scleranthus).
- Not able to hear or sense ones' inner knowing.
- Unable to trust own judgement – always asks others opinions.
- Personality often appears superficial to others.
- Blocked brow chakra.

It is vitally important that each of us is able to sense or hear our inner guidance (our connection to Source) and to be able to follow that, knowing it is Divine Will. Often, we are unaware that this is what we are doing. The way to recognise it is to see the Laws of the Universe in action when we follow Divine Will. When one is living in the moment the Law of Syncronicity comes into place and we start to recognise things happening just after we have thought about it. Action follows thought, another Divine Law. This is how we create our own reality. As Cerato is taken, one will find it easier to sense, feel or know that something is right for us. If one learns meditation or sits in stillness, taking ones consciousness to the heart, one can start to get a sense of knowing. In that silent space, one can ask questions of the higher self or receive guidance. Often one will hear a small still voice from within, or just a sense of knowing what to do. The secret is to TRUST THE FIRST THOUGHT or ANSWER you get when in that sacred space. This is coming from your spirit before your rational mind can interfere with the truth. The more we are able to follow our inner guidance and trust that we are supported by the Universe, the more we will feel our connection with Source.

Cherry Plum *Prenus Cerasifera*

CHERRY PLUM

POSITIVE QUALITIES

- Calm, poised and balanced in all circumstances.
- Mind, synchronised with true self. In control.
- Right and left brain working in harmony.
- Feeling sane and centred. Positive thoughts.

NEGATIVE STATES

- Fear of losing control, going insane or nervous breakdown.
- Sudden urges to commit violence to self or others.
- Suicidal feelings in the extreme state. Being on edge; jumpy.
- Screaming, shouting or no control over what you are saying.
- PMT symptoms. Wide open staring eyes.
- Character changes dramatically.

The negative Cherry Plum state can be likened to being in a car travelling at 100 m.p.h. with no-one at the steering wheel. The mind can be completely out of control or there is a great fear of that happening. When it happens you have no control at all over your thoughts, words and actions. Whatever is said or done at that time is usually deeply regretted afterwards, as often this state of mind comes and goes, often quite quickly. Those around you think you must have gone mad, unless they know and have these remedies to hand, in which case a few drops in a glass of water sipped will usually calm you down, it may have to be repeated, but often in an hour or less these crazy symptoms have left you. The Cherry Plum essence may be taken in this way, as the negative state manifests itself and can be seen to work very powerfully. This negative state often appears in women just before menstruation or for some people at full moon time, hence the term "lunatic". Indeed this flower essence would benefit many inmates of psychiatric hospitals, if it could be put into all their drinks, a great difference would be seen. (Any local health authorities wishing to try this approach, please apply to Heartsong for a donation of free essences). This state often appears when one is under a lot of pressure/stress. In its extreme form it can be suicidal feelings or the wish to harm the self or others, even loved ones. The negative state is often characterised by wide open, staring eyes, and words/actions which are totally out of character to the personality. Another way to work with this essence, if the negative state appears frequently or monthly, is to make up a dosage (see dosage instructions) bottle with a few other essences needed to balance the personality and take 6-8 times a day and keep repeating for weeks or months if necessary until the negative state no longer appears. This will very often clear this state of mind completely. I have seen great changes in clients over the years by using this method.

Chestnut Bud *Aeculus Hippocastanum*

CHESTNUT BUD

POSITIVE QUALITIES

- Ability to learn life's lessons.
- Able to mentally pick things up quickly.
- Can recognise that each experience or relationship has been drawn to you – so you can learn and grow.
- Students able to study more easily (see also Clematis).
- Fast inner growth.

NEGATIVE STATES

- Unable to learn and assimilate life's lessons through personal experience.
- Keep repeating the same mistakes over and over again.
- Unable to grasp things, ideas, quickly.
- Not able to retain information easily.
- Slow learners.
- Inability to study in a classroom situation.

Often people find it difficult to recognise that there is a lesson to be learnt from every situation or relationship in life. Indeed, the Law of the Universe helps us to do so by providing the Divine Law of Attraction. This means that we attract to us, whether we are conscious of it or not, patterns, situations, or people who are vibrating at the same frequency that we are giving out, to show or teach us some aspect of ourselves which we need to look at, something we need to change. This may be an attitude, an emotion, thought patterns or way of life. Often that person or situation is saying, "Do not choose this type of relationship again," or "Do not put yourself in this situation again, it causes you stress" etc. So, therefore we learn from this and either change our attitude, clear our emotions or get out of negative situations, whether it is a relationship, or in the workplace, etc. Then, we have recognised and grown from that which we have drawn to us and will no longer attract those experiences. Chestnut Bud needs to be taken when that learning does NOT take place. People stay stuck in destructive situations, or they keep repeating the same negative patterns time and time again. An example was an ex-client of mine, a lady who was continually attracting relationships with men who were either violent or were ill-treating her in some way. She said "I don't know why I keep doing this". This person obviously needed Centaury and other essences and I included Chestnut Bud in her combination bottle. After a few months of taking this mixture, she could see that she no longer needed to repeat this cycle, recognised what she needed to learn and moved on, feeling much happier. Life does not have to be a struggle or difficult if we understand Divine Truths and learn our lessons wisely. This essence is also good for students finding it difficult to study.

Chicory *Chichorium Intybus*

CHICORY

POSITIVE QUALITIES

- Can love others unconditionally.
- No strings attached or ties in relationships.
- Does not need company or others around.
- No emotional neediness.
- Gives others the freedom to be themselves.
- Does not feel the need to protect loved ones or direct their lives for them.
- No need for sympathy or attention.
- Earth Mother or Divine Mother energy.
- Open heart chakra.

NEGATIVE STATES

- Puts conditions on the love one gives.
- Emotional neediness, for company, sex, lovers or relationships.
- Selfishness. "The Needy Mother."
- Feels the need to control and direct loved ones; 'emotional blackmail.'
- Easily hurt or upset by others.
- Likes others to feel sorry for them, 'poor me'.
- Emotional security provided by money, possessions or relationships.
- Can cry very easily for attention and sympathy.
- Can evoke illness for the same reasons.
- Likes to be the centre of attention.
- Very talkative.

The characteristics of a person in need of Chicory flower essence are emotional neediness and lack of love. This is because deep within them they have lost the ability to love both themselves and others unconditionally. Hence, in relationships there are always strings attached to their love.

Often these strings are completely subconscious but nonetheless everyone around them can become enmeshed in a very unhealthy web of so called love. This love does not allow others to be themselves, as this person is always trying to guide and direct their "loved ones", and they feel it is for the other persons own good. In so doing, the object of their attention finds it very difficult to follow their own path and inner guidance. "Mother knows best', is one phrase that comes to mind, and indeed, the negative Chicory personality has long been represented as the "needy mother" figure. And indeed, if you have a mother like this, do also look to your own personality, as it is quite likely that you have taken on, subconsciously,

Chicory *Chichorium Intybus*

in childhood some of these aspects from mother as role model. This neediness can also be apparent from the need for possessions, collectors who fill their house with all sorts of things, as a replacement for love in their lives. The mother who does not want her grown-up children to leave home, the parent who tries to chain a child to her through ill-health, the person using sex as a tool to hang on to relationships, or as a barter system in marriage, giving favours to obtain what they want. These are all different scenarios in which the negative state of Chicory is displayed very well. Often, it is quite subtle, but it takes a good deal of will power and energy to not allow oneself to play into their emotional dramas. The personality displaying these symptoms usually feels that they are a very loving person, and indeed they are.

The love, however, is not a Divine, unconditional love but an emotional and conditional kind coming from the solar plexus rather than the heart chakra. As Chicory is taken, so the heart chakra is able to open more fully to display a more positive kind of energy, giving freedom to all and most of all the SELF. As we give others their freedom we gain our own.

CLEMATIS

POSITIVE QUALITIES

- Feeling very grounded and earthed.
- Able to be a part of the world.
- The ability to carry out tasks and function in an organised way.
- Will power and ability to focus the mind.
- Able to concentrate and study easily. Retentive memory.
- Good eyesight and hearing.
- Brings creativity from other dimensions to expression in the 3rd.
- Present, living in the NOW, attentive.

NEGATIVE STATES

- 'Ungrounded', not earthed. Very poor memory.
- Living in a fantasy world, in the future.
- Does not always hear, appears deaf.
- Eyesight often poor, accident prone.
- Unable to concentrate, focus or study.
- Dizzy spells, or losing consciousness.
- Cold hands and feet, often.
- Appears dreamy, often yawning, needs lots of sleep.
- Lack of energy, inattentive.

Clematis *Clematis Vitalba*

Often, during or after some kind of shock or trauma, the personality withdraws from the physical vehicle and takes its energies to other dimensions, the subtle levels. This is because it cannot deal with the pain, fears or emotions, at an earthly level. When one is fully present and grounded (or earthed) of course you feel all the emotional trauma, but that in one way, is essential to actually work through it and come out the other side, hence learning the lessons we came here to learn and becoming more emotionally clear and healed. This healing does not take place when ones energy withdraws to other dimensions. One becomes inattentive, withdrawn, ungrounded and "Not here". A vacant look is in the eyes and all energy is focused on fantasies, daydreams or other dimensional realities instead of this 3rd dimension worldly existence. This inability to deal with the present situation can easily be rectified by taking the Clematis flower essence. This helps one to be more focused, it is then easier to deal with and release what we have "switched off from", and live in the here and now, also to be more help to those around you. The other kind of negative Clematis state is where it is very deep-rooted stemming from childhood, or beyond, from previous incarnations spent meditating on mountain tops, or your higher self choosing for you to bring many fears into this life to be dealt with and cleared away, for your soul's growth. These are just some possibilities from the many clients I have seen needing Clematis in a more long term way, i.e. dosage bottle over many months. The readings I did for some of these people reveal those and many other situations where, effectively, in subtle energy terms, the base chakra closes down, making one ungrounded. The base chakra is the key to us living on the earth and fulfilling the role we came here to enact. This centre contains our basic instincts and often fears which we prefer not to look at and so we close this chakra down and become very ungrounded and unable to function in the world. As Clematis is taken so the centre opens, releasing any negativity it holds, into the auric field to be transmuted into positive energy. Often, a base chakra combination essence, the Inner Child essence Be Here Now or Mother Earth will be helpful at different stages of this process alongside Clematis.

Crab Apple *Malus Sylvestris*

CRAB APPLE

POSITIVE QUALITIES

- Feeling clean, healthy and pure.
- Unblemished skin, nails, radiates purity.
- Able to focus on the wider picture of life.
- Does not feel the need to be excessively clean.
- Psychic vacuum cleaner, transforming negativity of others.
- Not repulsed by dirt or dirty habits of others.

NEGATIVE STATES

- Feels unclean, impure or dirty, inside or out.
- Gets stuck in small details, fussy.
- Obsessive personality.
- Cleanliness fetish, needs lots of showers, washes.
- Houseproud, always cleaning.
- Blemished skin, skin complaints, acne.

Often the Crab Apple personality type is obsessed by the negative aspects in self and others, seeing it as somehow unclean or repulsive and dirty. They feel in some way not pure and are in fact, detached from the higher self aspect which knows there is purity and light in everything and everyone, regardless of how it appears outwardly. The inability to see this purity is often reflected in their own physical make-up, usually in a poor skin condition, acne, etc., which is showing the world that is the way they feel about themselves. "Action follows thought" is another Universal Law which we are all subject to. In this case, as we think of ourselves so we become, we create our own reality including our own physical body. The other aspects of this negative state are the obsessive qualities which become developed. This can show many forms, however, the most usual is some kind of cleanliness fetish. The need to wash or bath/shower excessively, continually washing ones hands. scrubbing the floor each day or obsessed by housework are all signs of the need for Crab Apple. Another manifestation is a fussy, negative attitude where too much attention is paid to small unimportant details. So much so that one loses the ability to see the wider view of a situation. This can show itself in many ways. Thus the personality can make mountains out of molehills in a seemingly ridiculous way. One client I treated many years ago was obsessed by housework and particularly by the need to shake a particular fur rug out in the garden many times each day, (again the obsession with small details). As I gave her Crab Apple in her combination essence, gradually over a period of several months she was able to let go of her fanatical cleaning. This lady was overjoyed when she came to a closing appointment and announced with a laugh, "I only shook the rug once last week." Also the shingles which she had developed as a manifestation of her own inner attitude to herself totally cleared up. Such is the healing power of Crab Apple.

Elm *Ulmus Procera*

ELM

POSITIVE QUALITIES

- Very capable.
- Let go and let God.
- Deals easily with responsibilities.
- Knows help will always be at hand.
- We are never given more than we can handle.
- Makes time for oneself.
- Adjusts easily to varying workload.

NEGATIVE STATES

- Feels overwhelmed.
- Responsibilities weigh heavily.
- Unable to cope with additional workload.
- Feels they will be unable to deal with extra burdens.
- Feels they will let others down.

Elm is one of the flower essences that is usually only needed in the short term. Often, in life, an extra responsibility is placed on our shoulders, or extra work in our career. Usually, the folks that need this essence are very capable people, able to deal easily with their chosen lot. Often, they hold down jobs with great responsibility, sometimes in management, or in charge of others, or in a home situation looking after a large family or an elderly/sick relative. It is when they suddenly feel that their burden is more than they can deal with and they feel overwhelmed by the situation that they need to take the Elm remedy, not when they are able to deal with those responsibilities easily. Often the essence will work very quickly in a matter of hours or days, other times it will need to go in a dosage bottle and be taken for several weeks; but gradually the person will start to feel lighter and will know that they are very capable and can easily deal with their situation. We can then recognise that help will always be at hand if we ask God/Universe for help and then TRUST.

Gentian *Gentiana Amarella*

GENTIAN

POSITIVE STATES

- Faith that all is working according to Divine Law.
- Trust that everything is in its right place. Optimistic personality.
- Knowing there is something better around the corner.
- Trust that one will always be supported by the Universe.

NEGATIVE STATES

- Negative personality. Not able to see positive aspects.
- Sceptical and pessimistic. Overly intellectual, too mental.
- Always asking too many questions. “Doubting Thomas” personality.
- Tries to understand with left brain, rather than developing inner knowing with the right brain.
- Lack of faith and trust in God/Universe.
- Easily disappointed at setbacks. Known depression.

The soul energy which is lacking in the negative Gentian type personality is the frequency of faith and trust. When we know without a doubt, in our heart (not just our head) that Mother/Father God always has our best interests at heart whatever the circumstances, we can never become disappointed, for we know then that higher Divine Laws are in operation and the outcome of any situation can only be for our soul’s growth. Usually, we cannot see this higher perspective as we are not easily able to project our lower personality to our higher self or I AM Presence unless we are spiritually of a high consciousness. So, we need the faith and trust to know that all is well at all times, even if not seemingly so at a lower level. This negative Gentian feeling can come at any kind of setback. Break-up of relationships, not getting particular work, bereavements, when in any way things do not seem to be going as planned. These plans usually take place at an ego level and therefore are often doomed to seeming failure. If we can learn to follow our higher self or spiritual guidance in all situations, everything starts to flow more freely. This can be learnt through meditation by putting the ego to one side. However, the guidance can only be followed when one has the faith and trust, knowing that it can only lead to good things, learning, growing, spiritual growth and happiness. Thus, the Gentian flower essence brings this soul quality into the consciousness, generating peace and transmuting doubts. Often, this is a very obvious long term remedy, but frequently it may be needed short term, after some kind of setback or disappointment. If in doubt whether this essence is needed, ask if the person becomes disappointed, if, for instance an important letter is not delivered on time or they do not get a job they really wanted, do they get depressed? If so, then the high vibrations of Gentian are needed for a more spiritual awareness and higher perspective on life.

Gorse *Ulex Europaeus*

GORSE

POSITIVE QUALITIES

- Retains a positive outlook on life in all circumstances.
- Always hopeful.
- Hope of healing in long-term illness.
- Does not become downhearted or depressed.
- Will always try one last thing to help them.

NEGATIVE STATES

- Feelings of hopelessness, given up hope.
- Dark rings around the eyes.
- Nothing can ever go right
- Despair and despondency
- Oh, what's the use?

In the negative Gorse state, the personality feels totally hopeless and despondent, thinks that no good can come from a situation. This state often appears in people subject to long term illness, or disease, when all hope has gone for a recovery. Often, this thought form is induced by doctors or specialists saying that nothing further can be done medically. This has, in my experience, been true of some patients with multiple sclerosis, arthritis and cancer. But something can be done from a complementary viewpoint and by the person taking Gorse flower essence a more positive outlook can be brought about which will allow, as Dr. Edward Bach discovered, the body's self healing process to activate itself. This great man knew, as Hippocrates, Paracelsus and Hanneman before him knew, disease and ill health are a by product of an unhealthy mind. If the personality becomes balanced on mental and emotional levels, the spirit can more easily bring healing energies through to the physical form. Positive thought forms produce a more positive body, we are and become, what we think, this is how we create our own reality. It is not only those with physical illness who are in need of Gorse. The need for this flower essence can often be spotted in extreme cases by dark circles around the eyes of the client. As the Gorse is taken, so its as if the sun comes out to dispel the darkness, just as the joyful yellow flowers are to be seen nearly all year round, to cheer and to heal us.

Heather *Calluna Vulgaris*

HEATHER

POSITIVE QUALITIES

- Good listener.
- Able to relate well to others with 2 way conversations.
- Can give and help others unselfishly.
- Has interest in others and things going on outside of themselves.

NEGATIVE STATES

- Over talkative.
- Hates to be alone, need continual attention.
- Cannot hear the words of others.
- Does not allow others a chance to talk.
- "Buttonholers" will push you into a corner and talk at you.
- Drain others at solar plexus by cording through emotional neediness.
- Often will develop ear problems.
- Totally, self-obsessed, often by their illnesses.
- They only talk about themselves.
- The "needy child".

The problem with the Heather personality is that at an ego level they are totally self-obsessed. They are only interested in what's going on for them and they often develop illnesses as proof of that obsession. They have even more to tell others and often go into great details about their operation, scars, wounds, sleep, etc. When they are in this negative state they are a bore to others, but they cannot stop talking long enough to hear if anyone tries to tell them. The fact is they are extremely poor listeners, only able to hear their own voice; therefore they often develop hearing difficulties as a way of them looking at the deeper meaning issues and healing themselves. The phrase "the needy child" is often used regarding this remedy type and indeed we can see similarities. Often we can trace this thought form back to childhood when there was some kind of deprivation whether emotional, mental or indeed, of love. As the Heather is taken so gradually the person is able to be silent long enough to hear others and they actually start to develop interests outside of themselves. I have seen this happen with many clients. It is wonderful to watch the transformation.

Holly *Ilex Aquifolium*

HOLLY

POSITIVE QUALITIES

- Inner peace. Kind nature.
- Open heart chakra, loving heart.
- Is not upset by others easily.
- Balanced sensitivity.
- Unconditional Love.

NEGATIVE QUALITIES

- Anger and rage, revengeful.
- Hatred, jealousy, and envy.
- Hard hearted, mean. Distrust of others.
- Suspicious and Over-sensitive.

Holly is a flower essence needed by many in western society. The culture of materialism seems to help generate the negative thought forms of Holly. We can look around and see it everywhere.

The housewife who is envious because her neighbour has electrical equipment bigger and better than hers, the husband who envies the managing director's large, powerful motor car.

The jealousy felt by the masses to someone who is seemingly better looking, more handsome or successful is fed by the media promoting consumer products. The feelings of hatred and revenge which have permeated down through civilisations, acted out by patriotism (which is misplaced as we are all global citizens), and wars. These energies stay around the earth plane as huge clouds and bands of negative thought forms which have to be cleared if the Earth is to progress to the new spiritual golden age of peace.

Anger is one of the most powerful energies we possess. When this force can be channelled in a positive way it unblocks our creative abilities and brings peace and calm. This is the power of the Holly essence which opens up the heart to Divine Love. As we feel this love more strongly, so the imbalances of anger, jealousy, revenge, etc., are released and transmuted. The beautiful holly flowers are the highest vibration of this spiky, and seemingly unfriendly tree. This then is it's signature, the transmutation of the lower ego states into open hearted love. The positive state of Holly is the most beautiful, powerful state of unconditional love. The love that encompasses all, even that which appears bad, evil or ugly, for all is one in the eyes of God and to love all is the most supreme state we can attain. A heart which is fully open, radiating love beholds beauty in everything and everyone; it heals and blesses all it touches.

Holly is one of the catalyst essences which can bring transformation to a 'stuck' case, or, where too many essences seem to be needed. Holly personality type can often have a red or angry complexion, and suffer extremes of heat. I have given Holly to women clients suffering from menopausal hot flushes and had remarkable results. Holly is also good in cases of fever and high temperature. A powerful essence for transformation of deep negative states.

Honeysuckle *Lonicera Caprifolium*

HONEYSUCKLE

POSITIVE QUALITIES

- Living in the here and now, the present.
- Not constantly talking about the past.
- Not thinking the past was better than now/future.
- Able to move on from traumatic happenings.

NEGATIVE STATES

- Mind locked into the past. Not living in the present.
- Wistfully looks back to happier times.
- Cannot forget loss of loved one. Many regrets.
- Feels homesick when going someplace different.
- Unable to let go of past trauma, bereavement, divorce, etc. (see also Star of Bethlehem).

When we need Honeysuckle flower essence, we are in some way locked into the past. The past could be yesterday or fifty years ago, the time lapse is not important. When the energy of our mind is focused on past events we are not able to be fully present in the here and now. What happens then is that we are not able to access the Divine energies as we are not synchronised with the Universe. When we are totally in the Now, fully here each moment, we are in tune, we can feel our intuition, inner guidance, access our Divine abundance, and doors can open for us on many levels. When our mind directs its energy to the past, all that movement stops, we no longer become a part of it.

The Ascended Masters I have channelled always stress the need to live in the moment if we are to grow. I have experienced this very directly as an exercise from my higher self. As I sat quietly after meditating, totally at peace, I was guided to think of the past, anything at all, as I did so after a few minutes I began to feel completely tense, my energies were not flowing. I asked what on earth is going on. I was told my feelings were directly attributed to my mind, (of course, but I had to be reminded of that) and my thoughts were the cause. Bringing myself back to present, my energy flowed again.

Sometimes, circumstances are such that it is difficult to stay focused on the present. Trauma, bereavement, are times when we cannot help thinking of our loved ones or happenings of the past. When moving house or emigrating it is hard not to feel that one is losing something or leaving part of ourselves behind in the old place. The elderly are often in need of this flower essence, as they have such strong memories and often feel unhappy with their life, change of circumstance or physical body now, so they continually think of the past and still live there, feeling it was better than the present. In truth, it usually was not, but the mind can find happy memories – even these can make one feel very sad and unhappy that things are no longer the way they were. As Honeysuckle is taken so the thoughts and sadness clear away. The memories will still be there when needed, it is the need to think of them that is gone!

Hornbeam *Carpinus Betulus*

HORNBEAM

POSITIVE QUALITIES

- Feels wide awake.
- Mental clarity.
- Enjoys breaks in routine and variety.
- Gets on with things needing to be done.
- Alert, and in the present.

NEGATIVE STATES

- Procrastination.
- 'Brain dead' or headachy after mental activity, reading, computer, television.
- Monday morning feeling.
- Too much routine in life, no spontaneity.
- Mental tiredness, weariness, sluggish mind.
- Not fully awake.
- Needs time or coffee in morning, before feeling alert.
- Students unable to study, tired.

Hornbeam refreshes the mind, bringing more mental alertness. This flower essence is often used in the short term or for an immediate wake-up feeling.

Sometimes when we wake up in the morning we are not able to be totally awake, the mind procrastinating over things to be done that day and often a feeling of not being able to get on and carry out those tasks. This feeling can also come about after much mental work, or sitting in front of a computer for the day. In these cases, again, use the simple, immediate solution. If this is an occasional feeling, then a few drops of Hornbeam flower essence in a drink and then sipped, or directly on the tongue, will soon have you alert and awake, able to go forward into the day happily. If this feeling persists or is a continual way of being then the Hornbeam needs to be taken in a dosage bottle 6-8 times a day until the feeling disperses. The time span could be days, weeks or a month or more depending on how long you have been in that frame of mind.

Hornbeam is good for people who live an unbalanced lifestyle; usually folks who are using their mental abilities, (left brain, masculine), far more than their creative, intuitive abilities, (right brain, feminine.) This can bring a dull kind of weariness, a brain dead feeling. When in this state it is easy to feel that one will not be able to accomplish that which needs to be done, and therefore procrastinate, keep putting things off. If living very much on the mental plane it is good to balance the lifestyle to stimulate energy.

When in this mental state of lethargy and procrastination, again, one is out of the Now, being in this moment, alive, alert and able to focus on what needs to be done next. As Hornbeam is taken it allows one to come back to that pure, positive state of clear mental energy.

Impatiens *Impatiens Glandulifera*

IMPATIENS

POSITIVE QUALITIES

- Patient and calm.
- Independent nature.
- Quick thinking with a lively mind.
- Able to work with others easily.
- Knows there is time for everything.
- Allows others time and space.

NEGATIVE STATES

- Impatient and irritable.
- Lot of inner tension.
- Sudden, sharp pains or indigestion.
- Expects everything to happen 'yesterday'.
- Frustrated by life and others.
- Says 'It's quicker to do it myself'.
- Easily flares up, quick tempered.
- Likes to work alone as others, slower, irritate.
- Walks and talks too quickly.
- Finishes others sentences for them.
- Always wants to get on to the next thing.

It is relatively easy to identify when one is in need of Impatiens flower essence. Everything is done very quickly, whether it be work, leisure, walking, talking. Even just being, you will find the Impatiens type personality, foot tapping, unable to sit still. Often their impatience will get the better of them and they will flare up in temper, often at others who are, in their mind, too slow. This temper is very short lived, unlike Holly type anger, and soon fades away, forgotten. Often, if they give someone else a job to do, they will watch out of the corner of their eye and if the work is not being done quickly enough, they will soon be wanting to push the person out of the way and will take over themselves. "I can do it quicker" is an often heard phrase. An Impatiens type will walk very quickly so others find it difficult to keep up with them. They also talk at an alarming speed, and, especially if trying to teach others, their words will often be incomprehensible.

I have often given Impatiens for pain relief, as we can all get tense and frustrated that we are not recovering fast enough. Impatiens, like Holly, can also be useful for helping to reduce fevers and hot flushes.

As Impatiens is taken over a period of time, for this state of mind is often deep rooted, the person will gradually become calmer in themselves, and with a more relaxed frame of mind will often accomplish more than with impatient activity. The tension stored in their body, often in head and shoulders disappears. They will also find it easier to work with others, becoming a calmer and happier companion.

Larch *Larix Decidua*

LARCH

POSITIVE QUALITIES

- Confident outlook on life.
- Ability to tackle new projects.
- No fears of failure.
- Limitless, broadens ones horizons.
- Feels equal to all others.

NEGATIVE STATES

- Lack of self-confidence.
- Feels inferior to others.
- Expects failure so stops trying.
- Self limiting. Often says 'I can't'.
- Feelings of impotency.
- Fears of failure (also see Mimulus).
- Feels one is not as capable as others.
- Does not attempt new things.

Larch flower essence helps us to develop self-confidence. When one is lacking this attribute, life can often be an ordeal, as often the simplest things can become difficult with this negative attitude. When one is afraid to move forward, take on a new occupation, form relationships, etc. one can become completely stuck and not able to learn and grow from these situations on our life's path. Lack of confidence within oneself will eventually lead to the personality not even attempting anything new for fear of either not being good enough or of failure.

A Larch character will look around at others and admire the way they sail through life and accomplish things, wishing they could be the same. They are never envious of others, however, and usually stand back allowing others with more confidence to move forward. One can best see Larch types in the classroom, but can easily be seen later in life, the trait having become deep-rooted. As the Larch flower essence is taken so the natural confidence that we all carry, deep within us, is able to emerge and carry us forward in life in a more positive way.

Mimulus *Mimulus Guttatus*

MIMULUS

POSITIVE QUALITIES

- Brave and courageous.
- No fear of any known thing.
- Happy in group situations.
- Able to speak freely with others.

NEGATIVE STATES

- Fears of known things. i.e. spiders, heights, water, driving, money and phobias.
- Reserved, shy, over-sensitive to others.
- Over-sensitive to environment, anger, conflict, swearing, aggression.
- Nervous laughter or over-talkative, to cover up embarrassment.
- Shyness and timidity, blushes easily.
- Stammer or stuttering. Not happy in group situations.
- Sensitive to noise and bright lights. Easily startled.

The Mimulus type personality is easily identified. As they carry so much anxiety and fear they are nervous, shy, timid but gentle creatures. The fears tend to rule their whole life making many things others would consider normal, almost impossible to achieve. Taking a driving test or studying for examinations, going to the dentist or on holiday can all become nightmares, which many Mimulus types will not even attempt. These fears are always of known things and the origins are often traceable. Some, however are not so. One lady I treated had a great fear of birds, especially black ones. This fear could not be traced in this life so I looked into her akashic records, (soul memory) during a session and was shown a picture of her being imprisoned in the Tower of London where the ravens were continually flying in and around her cell. I did not need to see the rest of that lifetime, it was enough. I then gave the karmic fear essence of Pink Rose, which cleared it; but only after a few months of Mimulus had shifted other fears but not this deep-rooted past life one.

Another client was terrified of going on an aeroplane and after taking Mimulus for a while, she calmly came for an appointment and happily announced she finally felt able to go abroad and had booked her first ever flight. I gave her some Emergency Essence to take on the plane, and when she returned she shared that she had given it to others but needed little herself.

A fear of thunderstorms can often be traced to childhood. In Victorian times many children were shut under the stairs during storms because of their own or their parent's fears. One client could clearly remember this happening to her but the knowledge or memory was not enough to release the fear. As the Mimulus is taken so the fears gradually diminish as the individual's innate courage surfaces.

So Mimulus is used to treat any kind of physical fear or anxiety. For unknown fears, look to Aspen, strong fears, terror to Rock Rose. A person may have a sudden fear which arises of any known thing and yet not be the timid type typical of needing the essence. Then Mimulus is taken short term to clear away the fears very quickly.

Mustard *Sinapis Arvensis*

MUSTARD

POSITIVE QUALITIES

- Bright and sunny disposition.
- Positive outlook.
- Unaffected by the weather, grey or sunny.
- Head feels clear and light.

NEGATIVE STATES

- Gloom or depression which comes and goes for no reason.
- No logical reason for this state, unlike Gentian.
- No control over this gloom, disappears of it's own accord.
- Unable to express this mood or cover it up.
- Dark cloud hanging over ones head.
- Headaches, heavy headed.

Like Gorse, the Mustard flowers brings the sunshine brilliance of yellow to disperse gloom and depression. Unlike Gorse, however, which usually has a known cause, the negative Mustard state comes along for no apparent reason. The feelings of gloom and despondency seem to hang around and above the head like a dark heavy cloud. Again for no reason it disappears, and so it comes and goes at odd times, casting its spell of depression. As the Mustard essence is taken so the life force of the small yellow flowers dispels the negative state, just as Edward Bach described the sun dispelling the clouds in the sky. Often Mustard is only needed in the short term and a few drops in a drink or two will be enough to chase the clouds away. If, however, the Mustard state is one that appears regularly for you, it is important to add it to a combination bottle and take it regularly for a month or two. This is often long enough to release that pattern from one's mind permanently.

Do not confuse Mustard with Gentian. Gentian is always for known depression or disappointment, whereas there seems to be no reason for the Mustard state of gloom.

This feeling can be a headachy or heavy headed sense and is, again, completely different from the headaches or migraines often suffered by those needing the Vervain essence.

Oak *Quercus Robur*

OAK

POSITIVE QUALITIES

- Strong and resilient, great endurance.
- Reliable, never gives up.
- Respected by others.
- Makes time for oneself.
- Recognises the need to work as a joy, not a duty.
- Withstands the greatest of tests.
- Able to carry heavy burdens.
- Strength inspires others.
- Strong physical body.

NEGATIVE STATES

- Strength suddenly ebbs away.
- Unable to carry on.
- Great weariness.
- Bravely fights on, enduring much.
- Makes no time for own relaxation.
- Lower physical body in pain, often back, hips or legs.

The Oak tree exemplifies strength and fortitude. It is the strongest tree in the woods, sheltering smaller, weaker trees under its strong, spreading branches. One can rest under its shelter, and lean on or hug its broad trunk and feel its energy and healing qualities, coming away feeling refreshed, and somehow stronger. It is this quality of fortitude which is restored by taking the Oak flower essence. This powerful remedy is only needed at the very time when one is unable to continue, feeling almost at a point of physical/mental breakdown. The mental thought pattern is somehow reflected in a lack of physical energy, often with the legs giving way. I personally have taken this essence frequently, being an Oak type, often I first notice I need it when my back feels overburdened and painful. As I sip the Oak in a drink so my energies are restored and pains disappear. The Oak type personality can be likened to the tree itself, big and strong, helping and sheltering other life forms, until suddenly for no reason, its roots become weakened and often the whole tree can topple down. It is only at this stage that the person needs to take the flower essence and the life force of the tree, captured in the living water, renews us and restores our strength.

The Oak personality type is greatly relied upon by others and is often a leader, or carrying large responsibilities. Their positive strength and fortitude can uphold nations, especially in times of trouble. One example of this may be Sir Winston Churchill in the second world war; his positive energy was a great source of strength and helped the British people to have hope in their hearts.

Olive *Olea Europapaea*

OLIVE

POSITIVE QUALITIES

- Physical and mental strength.
- Great energy.
- Knowing we can access Universal energy.
- Strong auric field.

NEGATIVE STATES

- Physical tiredness and exhaustion.
- Mental tiredness.
- Too tired to do anything.
- Energy depleted on all levels.
- Working too hard.
- Energy reserves drained after illness.

Olive is another of those flower essences often needed just at the right moment. Time spent in the garden digging, for example, and them coming indoors and realising how tired we have become. A lot of physical/mental work in any way at all can result in feelings of exhaustion or tiredness. Even on holiday, when a day spent driving, sightseeing or walking around can bring about the need to take the Olive essence. Again, at these times it is often enough to take just a few drops in a glass of water or cup of tea and in a very short time ones energy is restored, often without noticing the change. Suddenly, one feels able to get up to do something and realises the subtlety of the workings of these precious gifts of nature.

Olive can also be needed more as a longer term energy restorative. At times when ones reserves of energy have been drained, for example, long term disease or illness can be extremely debilitating or overworking for long periods of time can also deplete our energy and sap our strength. At these times, it is important to take the Olive in a dosage bottle, usually with other essences, 8 times a day until one feels restored and replenished. Olive flower essence is a wonderful, natural aid to convalescence and to everyday life.

Pine *Pinus Sylvestris*

PINE

POSITIVE QUALITIES

- Self-worth.
- All beings are equal.
- Knowing you are innocent.
- Self forgiveness.
- Feeling your connection with Source.

NEGATIVE STATES

- Guilt feelings.
- Always needing to apologise.
- Feels always in the wrong.
- Feels responsible for others mistakes, takes the blame.
- Self accusation and reproach.
- Strong ideas of 'sin', especially regarding sexuality.
- One could always have done something better.
- Feels unworthy, puts oneself last.
- Others are more deserving.

The disassociation from Source which the Pine flower essence corrects is one where the Soul quality of self worth is not present or not able to come through to personality level. When one feels lacking in this essential virtue, there is again stagnation in growth. The huge negative thought form of guilt stems from this feeling of lack of worthiness. In essence, it is stemming from our very first incarnations on the Earth plane when we started to develop ego and then felt we did not deserve connection with Source. This brought about in the earthly human mind a feeling of guilt at not being connected totally to the creative force, as we were before we took on physical incarnations.

Guilt is one of the most damaging thought forms on the Earth today, along with fear. Guilt has continued to be perpetuated in humans since that time through persecutions, churches and religions which have perpetuated the myth of guilt, as we are "sinners", who have reinforced within us that we are incapable of feeling Source/God within us and therefore are not connected. They have chosen to make themselves powerful by saying you can only reach God through another human being, priest, clergy, etc. So throughout the ages our unworthiness has loomed larger and larger in our human eyes, until we can no longer recognise that we are all divine sparks from the creative force carrying our own light. Even more so, we can connect directly to Source in meditation and stillness without any outside interference. Even more importantly, as many are now discovering, we are also masters in our own right, and when we are clear and totally aligned to our light and true self, healing energies come through and even miracles may start to happen. For those who have feelings of guilt and unworthiness, the Pine flower essence will bring back the connection and the knowing that you are divine beings.

For further reading see the Course in Miracles.

Red Chestnut *Aesculus Carnea*

RED CHESTNUT

POSITIVE QUALITIES

- Knowing all are safe.
- Able to send healing thoughts to those they love.
- No fears for family or friends.
- Trusting everything is in its right place.

NEGATIVE STATES

- Fears for others.
- Afraid harm may come to others.
- Always imagines the worst.
- Say's "They must have had an accident" if late.
- Excessive attachment to loved ones through fear.
- Anxiety for friends and family.

When a person is in the negative Red Chestnut state, there is a lack of trust that others are all well in the Divine plan, a lack of acceptance that whatever may happen to them it has a purpose. Hence, a great fear that others may come to harm, especially loved ones and people one knows closely. In this state, there is however, no fear for oneself, only the overriding fear that something dreadful will happen to others. This fear may be projected by a housewife, waiting for her husband to come home. If he is late she will immediately feel that some great harm has come to him, she will be watching the clock and with the passing time, the disaster that has befallen him will become greater and greater until eventually she may even start phoning relatives or the local hospital, saying "He must have had an accident!" When he eventually returns, the fear immediately disappears until next time. The mother fearing for her child who is outside playing, having to watch him each moment to ensure no harm comes to him.

Men also, of course can suffer the Red Chestnut state, it is not only related to women. One man I treated had a wife with severe arthritis, and although he was ill himself with asthma, he had no fear for himself, only that his wife would suffer terribly and end up in a wheelchair. At work, during the day, his mind would be filled with fears of her doing herself some harm at home. As he took the Red Chestnut along with other essences he needed, gradually these fears diminished and his asthma greatly improved – another example of our thoughts creating illness, "we are what we think."

The positive state of Red Chestnut is that of the world's greatest healers. The ability to send healing thoughts and unconditional love from the heart to those they care for; knowing the other person is safely enfolded in Mother/Father God's Divine Love and that each is moving through life's circumstances according to the great Divine plan. By removing ones ego, (the fear), when sending healing one can ask for it to work according to that persons highest Divine good, without attachment to a particular result; knowing that whatever the outcome, ALL IS WELL, for that persons growth.

Rock Rose *Helianthemum Nummularium*

ROCK ROSE

POSITIVE QUALITIES

- Calmness in all situations.
- Sleeps deeply and undisturbed.
- Able to help others in emergencies.

NEGATIVE STATES

- Terror and very strong fear.
- Shaking, heart stopping fear.
- Panics in emergencies.
- Nightmares.
- Panic attacks.

Rock Rose is a very extreme negative state to be in. When one is in a state of terror, panic or extreme fear, ones whole being seizes up and one becomes unable to function comfortably on any level. Sometimes this state is brought about by an emergency situation of some kind, an accident, trauma, etc. In these situations, if one person is terrified or panicking it also affects those around including any casualties of an accident thus hindering their self-healing process. Fear vibrations set up a very strong etheric density which is experienced by others (whether consciously or subconsciously, depending on their levels of sensitivity). These waves of energy can then trigger off fears in the minds of others and in very extreme situations can set off mass hysteria. As we become more aware of how our energies affect others, through our auric field, we start to become conscious of the need to change our negative though forms into positive ones. In these extreme circumstances, Rock Rose or the Emergency Essence Combination (which contains Rock Rose), given to all those involved calms the whole energy field down, restoring calm and bringing order to the situation.

Often however, Rock Rose needs to be taken over a period of time in a dosage bottle, to clear and transmute those negative patterns. Anyone who suffers panic attacks, strong fears or nightmares on a regular basis needs this treatment. Gradually, the fears recede and the person starts to function in a calmer manner. One client I had, came to see me for treatment of panic attacks. He was experiencing these almost every day and was not sleeping well, often suffering nightmares. When I looked at his aura, I saw not just the jagged and uneven surface common to persistent drug/alcohol abusers but holes in his etheric body which were allowing all sorts of negative impressions into his physical and subtle bodies and which were then affecting his mind, the crown and solar plexus chakras being particularly affected. I gave him some healing and essences including Rock Rose and told him to take them 8 times a day. I saw him after one week and he had already started changing. Over the next few months he stayed on flower essences and I also introduced Larimar, a gem remedy to repair the damaged aura, along with more healing. He very quickly became a changed person, calm, sleeping well and developing into a good healer himself.

Rock Water *Aqua Petra*

ROCK WATER

POSITIVE QUALITIES

- Kind and loving towards oneself.
- Highest ideals become reality.
- Open mind to new ideas and possibilities.
- Does not need to be an example to others, so becomes a very positive one.
- Has flexible attitude to life and self.

NEGATIVE STATES

- Rigid attitude towards self.
- Forces oneself to become a martyr.
- Often ignores the world and enjoyment in worldly things.
- Wishes to change others through their rigid example.
- Strict and rigid views on the 'right' way, often related to spiritual disciplines.
- Deeply suppressed emotional or physical needs.
- Self-disciplinarian, perfectionist.
- Very strict in lifestyle, diet, etc.
- Denies oneself any luxury or simple pleasure.

The personality of Rock Water type when in a negative state is needing to learn lessons in flexibility of the mind. In this pattern the person is very rigid and controlling of themselves and particularly their lifestyle. They develop these patterns as an extreme way of showing others how good they are, hoping to change others to their way of thinking. This can be seen in many ways, some of the most common are these, a very rigid diet and strict abstinence from alcohol, coffee, etc. By enforcing this upon themselves they hope to influence and change the diet etc. of those around them. They do not realise that this lifestyle would possibly come about naturally as a raising of consciousness, as one becomes more sensitive so one no longer desires these substances. By enforcing it rigidly on oneself, playing the martyr, it is a quite unhealthy thought pattern, however healthy the regime. This personality is regarded as the "sackcloth and ashes" type, always ensuring a rigid, very hard lifestyle for themselves. They will deny all "luxuries" for themselves and often even necessities like warmth and decent clothing. What they do not realise is that this self denial and wishing to change others cannot possibly work. Others may often be changed in some way by our example but only if that example is from love, love for ourselves and others, not through self denial or rigidity. These extreme though patterns also can contribute to rigidity of the body, such as arthritis, back pain, etc. As the Rock Water essence is taken so their minds and bodies become more supple and flowing and free from pain.

Scleranthus *Scleranthus Annuus*

SCLERANTHUS

POSITIVE QUALITIES

- Decisive and positive.
- Well balanced.
- Emotional and mental balance.
- Able to choose easily between two things.

NEGATIVE STATES

- Indecisive.
- Unable to choose between two things.
- Tries to decide alone, (unlike Cerato).
- Mind like a grasshopper, jumps from one subject to another.
- Often late for appointments, appears unreliable to others.
- Travel sickness, inner ear imbalance.
- When ill, illness or pain comes and goes or moves position.
- Unbalanced emotionally.
- Jerking movements, physically off-balance.
- Extremes of behaviour, erratic.
- Mood swings.

The Scleranthus type typifies the unbalanced, indecisive character. When in this negative state it becomes very difficult to choose, when the decision is to be made between two things. (Do not confuse with Cerato, unable to decide between many choices). This indecision is caused by an imbalance in the left and right brain, lack of synchronicity, often felt as earache or an inner ear imbalance, vertigo, etc. This shows itself more easily as travel sickness, when one is unable to be at ease with the motion of a boat, train or car. This is only because the self is out of balance so it cannot synchronise with the motions of movement.

The Scleranthus type can suffer extremes of temperament. The mood can change as easily as the weather from happiness, joy to moodiness, or despair, etc. This again is showing the unbalanced mind.

As the Scleranthus essence is taken so one develops a more balanced and centred personality. This is reflected in the ability to be able to choose very easily between two things, the highs and lows become evened out, and the travel sickness, vertigo, unbalanced walking, etc. (the physical signs of the need for this remedy) disappear. One lady I treated had severe Multiple Sclerosis and had great difficulty walking, always losing her balance, she was also very indecisive. When she took Scleranthus her walking became greatly improved, when it was left out of her combination bottle, it deteriorated again. After staying on Scleranthus a long time, she became balanced on all levels. Thus the energy and life force of the tiny Scleranthus flower helps to bring balance to our lives.

Star of Bethlehem *Ornithogalum Umbellatum*

STAR OF BETHLEHEM

POSITIVE QUALITIES

- Calm and poised.
- Able to deal with shocks, traumas easily.
- Unruffled in emergencies.

NEGATIVE STATES

- In a state of shock.
- Past or recent accident or trauma in life.
- Sudden news upsets one.
- Energy blocks caused by past trauma.

Star of Bethlehem is the antidote to any kind of shock, trauma, upset or bad news. Shock resonates through ones system causing many difficulties in mind, emotions and body. Shock waves can completely block the body's own ability to heal itself and throws the mind and emotions into total chaos. If Star of Bethlehem is taken immediately the incident happens it greatly reduces these problems and one is able to heal and continue life in a balanced way. This flower essence is needed under many different circumstances, from loss of a loved one through divorce or bereavement, receiving bad news, or in an accident, hospitals, operations, and many more. If these situations are not treated at the time, their vibrations stay locked into the system until they are either resolved at a later stage when one is more able to deal with the trauma, or they eventually take their toll on the physical body. One such circumstance may be when extreme shock or trauma happened in childhood, whether parents separated, war-time situations, abuse of any kind, even a child being suddenly moved from home and school, uprooted from everything known can cause extreme trauma, even if it is not able to be expressed at the time. I have known people with childhood trauma to be able to release it and speak of it, often for the first time, much later in life, after taking Star of Bethlehem flower essence. Even the trauma of birth stays locked into the system, as anyone involved in re-birthing knows, until it is released. Experienced healers know that these childhood shocks and even trauma from past incarnations, are held at a cellular level in the body's memory. I have had many clients that have released long-held difficulties from the body during a healing session. It takes many forms, shaking, sudden jolts, a pain or trapped nerves being released as well as often the emotional trauma; tears are sometimes a part of this sacred healing process leaving the person at peace. Because Star of Bethlehem is such an important flower essence it is included in the Emergency Combination and therefore is one of the most essential of all the 38. This essence may also be used as a catalyst when a block or plateau is reached in ones healing process. Star of Bethlehem or Emergency Essence is an invaluable tool for this transformational process.

Sweet Chestnut *Castanea Sativa*

SWEET CHESTNUT

POSITIVE QUALITIES

- Each day a new opportunity for growth.
- Strength and light coming from the soul.
- Restored and renewed.
- The energy to move forward spiritually, to next stage of growth.
- At peace with one's self.

NEGATIVE STATES

- The dark night of the soul.
- Deep, dark depression.
- Despair, utter hopelessness.
- Feeling lost and in the dark.
- Total desolation, feels like the end of the road.
- Isolated from one's spirit, lack of soul connection.
- The storm before the calm.
- Despair and darkness.
- Alone in the Universe.

These beautiful hanging flowers of light symbolise the light of the soul, coming down from Source and entering physical realms and the mind through the higher self connection. The creamy white flowers bringing forth energy to later fruit and provide sweet food in the form of the chestnut, just as the higher spiritual energies give food and nourishment to the lower personality. This will eventually crack open the outer shell, (or the ego's defence mechanisms), to allow further growth from within.

We all, at one time or another in our lives, need to experience this feeling of total desolation. We need this opportunity to come to the realisation that all things, thoughts and feelings are only passing; and even these extreme thought patterns of the negative Sweet Chestnut state are showing us that there is light at the end of the tunnel. The light of course being our own soul illumination which is always there, it is just sometimes covered up by our thoughts and emotions.

On the one occasion when I experienced this extreme negative state, (after realising that it was the one essence of all 38 that I had never needed and asking my higher self to allow me the privilege of knowing how my clients felt in this state), I felt totally isolated, alone in the whole universe, surrounded by darkness and disconnected from Source with no way out. I was driving my car at the time and managed to get home to take some essences. Suddenly, I realised this was what I had prayed for the day before. A few drops on my tongue and in a drink and the whole

Vervain *Verbena Officianalis*

mood of darkness passed away, I was once again in the light. Others have described the feeling as being in a tunnel, box or in a dark room, devoid of all light as if disconnected from ones true being.

The negative Sweet Chestnut state is also known as the "dark night of the soul", and it is often that after going through this deep, transformational experience a rebirth takes place. So this state often comes at times of deep change and transformation in our life and is, often, a necessary precursor to spiritual growth and renewal. Almost like a last ditch attempt by the ego to prevent the light from transforming it. Many lightworkers will recognise these symptoms as stages of raising vibratory frequencies, when much healing takes place. I have noticed in some clients there is deep karmic clearance taking place when they are needing this essence.

Just as the ancient Egyptians had the symbol of the scarab for spiritual renewal, so the essence of Sweet Chestnut can be likened to the dung beetle of Egypt. As this flower essence is taken, so light, joy and understanding flood the mind, taking one to a new stage of the life journey.

VERVAIN

POSITIVE QUALITIES

- Positive enthusiasm for life.
- A great inspiration to others.
- Working positively to Divine Will.
- Able to see others views and opinions.
- Enjoys work in balanced way.
- No desire to change others.
- Mind and body relaxed.
- Gives time for oneself.
- Sacral chakra balanced.

NEGATIVE STATES

- Very tense and stressed, highly strung.
- Overworks, hyper-activity, unable to relax.
- Gets extremely over excited, over the top.
- Burn themselves out through over use of will.
- Over exhausted, tension in head and body, headaches or migraine.
- Over enthusiastic, over stimulated.
- Perfectionist, nothing ever right.
- Wishes to change the world, convert others to their beliefs.
- Fanatical, incensed by injustices.
- Overzealous, missionary type.
- Always on the go.

The Vervain personality type carries a lot of fire energy. When used positively this energy can transform and inspire others to their highest potential, can bring great changes to the earth through the righting of injustices and support of humanitarian causes. Many of those involved in the 'green' or peace organisations, or helping animals and refugees are achieving positive effects through the inspiration of their Higher Self, followed by the use of Divine Will in conjunction with the energy of love. They know that one cannot inflict one's own will on others for any reason whatsoever, however bad one may consider the other person or their views. We can only transform any situation by being open to the opinion of others, with the recognition that each is entitled to their own view, just as each is learning or growing through different experiences on their path, which may be different to ours. In an attitude of love and brotherhood we can best heal the rifts that divide, and so bring peace and harmony to the world.

This comes through a release of the negative state of Vervain, the need to fight for causes and over use of the ego's will; thus bringing more inner peace which is then reflected out into the world, so creating outer peace.

Vervain, then, is for those people who over strive, always trying very hard in whatever they do, causing much stress mentally with lots of inner tension and strain on the physical body. In this negative frame of mind they are constantly wishing to change the thought patterns and behaviour of others and can become quite angry when their ways of 'helping' others fails. They will try to force their own views and ideas onto others, thinking it is for the good of that person, even when that person is very obviously not interested, the Vervain type can become so obsessed they will try to drive home their point of view.

The Vervain personality type can be quite fanatical in their belief structures. Due to their extreme natures, however, they usually have little impact on global transformation until their behaviour becomes more moderate and balanced. The individuals most helping to change the planet are those who are in the balanced Vervain state, putting their ideas into workable methods, whether economically, politically or with humanitarian causes.

The recognition that all change first comes from within, by changing ones own thought forms and responses to others and the world, so we make the changes from a point of balance and inner peace. These changes can never come from a place of anger and tension (the negative Vervain state). Vervain individuals are very highly strung, driving and pushing themselves to go beyond their limits, whatever they are doing. Therefore they become exhausted and very stressed out. They appear to be quite extreme, or can easily get over excitable and over the top. They often have a perfectionist attitude, needing everything to be exact. As Vervain is taken so they become more relaxed in mind and body, releasing their inner tension, which can frequently be the cause of headaches.

VINE

POSITIVE QUALITIES

- Good leadership skills, open to opinions of others.
- Respected by others.
- Energy used for the good of all.
- Able to serve others.
- Inner power is balanced.
- No desire to control others.

NEGATIVE QUALITIES

- Very dominant and strong willed.
- Always know they are right.
- Tyrant who persecutes others.
- Always wants things done their way.
- Strongly ambitious, needing power and control.
- Rules with a rod of iron.
- Rides roughshod over others.
- Can be ruthless in business.
- Authoritarian, inflexible and rigid.
- The child bully in the playground, over strict parent, tough boss.
- A "power freak".
- Bossy and controlling.

Those individuals carrying the Vine personality type have come into this life to learn about control and the most important lesson for their souls growth is that of balanced power. This personality has within its energy field the capacity for powerful, balanced and good leadership. These are the "born leaders", captains of industry, politicians, or simply good leaders of men. They are able to hear others, listen to differing views and make sound judgements.

This energy field goes out of alignment if the ego becomes too fond of the power the spirit and soul are bringing through to the lower personality. The ego then uses this strength to control and dominate others, riding roughshod over others less powerful than themselves. We can see these characteristics in the cruel tyrant, or the dominant bully. There is no consideration for their fellow man, simply a strong, egotistical knowing that they are right, therefore everyone else must follow their will and be under their control. Egotism at its most strongest!

In relationships, the negative Vine personality, (strong willed), usually attracts to it a negative Centaury person, (weak willed), so that in the relationship each can learn lessons for their growth. The Centaury type, if at all aware, will learn to stand up to the partner and not be such a doormat. The Vine person will learn to be more gentle and less dominant. If this growth does not take place, eventually, after many years the Centaury type may find their own inner strength and leave the relationship.

Vine *Vitis Vinifera*

We see these attractions of opposites in all walks of life, business, friendships and marriage. As people become more aware of the spiritual Divine Laws that govern the Universe, so they will be more aware of the Law of Opposites. The Law is in operation to reinforce learning through the polarities. The dual nature of the Earth is evolving to a point where there will be no dark/light, good/bad etc. simply a point of balance in the middle, with the knowing that everything just IS. This point comes from a place of non-judgement and recognition of the Laws of Karma, where each is learning and growing through duality consciousness. The largest shift of consciousness on the planet will come with the mass recognition that there is a choice of DIVINE LOVE instead of FEAR, this being the polarisation that has taken humanity to the extremes we have experienced recently and through many ancient civilisations where much learning and growth has taken place regarding the misuse of power. The most important of these was Atlantis and although the earth has almost reached the point of destruction the Atlanteans reached, the tide of consciousness has now turned enough to avoid such a catastrophe again. This use of power is the lesson for all Vine types to conquer with the help of the gentle but powerful Vine flowers.

WALNUT

POSITIVE QUALITIES

- The Link Breaker.
- Adaptable and supple.
- Moves easily through changes, finding them exciting.
- Unaffected by the energy of others.
- Complete release of the past.
- Constant and true to oneself.
- Flows easily through life, flexible.
- Open to new opportunities.

NEGATIVE QUALITIES

- Resistant to change.
- Oversensitive.
- Too open to frequencies of others.
- Feels like a layer of skin is missing.
- Easily becomes tired and drained around others.
- Cannot adapt to new situations and change.
- Gets stuck in periods of transition.
- Weak and sensitive aura and solar plexus.
- Feels too open, unprotected.

Walnut *Juglans Regia*

There are many times in life when the subtle energy of Walnut flower essence is needed. Walnut assists with all kinds of life changes and situations. The most obvious being times of great trauma, bereavement and divorce. At these times, great stages of growth can be obtained on our life path by being able to move through these times of transition feeling unhindered by upset, emotion and inflexibility. During these severe movements Walnut can bring ease and balance, being especially powerful in combination with Star of Bethlehem to release the trauma/shock and Honeysuckle to release the past.

Walnut is also helpful for new born babies, infants when teething, learning to walk, etc., children starting a new school, during puberty, when first married or pregnant, moving house, new job, or to help menopausal changes.

Another time this mixture is of great help is at our last stage of transition in physical bodies, the dying process. At this time it is often good to include a fear essence in the combination, Aspen is usually indicated but Mimulus, Rock Rose, Cherry Plum can also be needed, depending on the personality; or Red Chestnut if our greater fear is for those we leave behind.

In truth we are all Divine beings of light who exist multi-dimensionally, the earthly existence being the lowest and densest in the vibratory scale. As we raise our conscious awareness of other states of existence through meditation, prayer and other spiritual practises so we come to know our true nature as eternal. As we leave this world and body behind, so we take on a new and lighter form and continue our existence on other levels. The transition can be as easy or difficult as we have "chosen" to make it, depending on our lessons necessary for our souls growth. Beautiful angels, beings of light and often, loved ones who have already passed over, are all awaiting to assist us on the "other side", (the 4th dimension of consciousness). Walnut and other flower essences are one of the most important tools at these times of transition and are becoming very widely used in hospices.

Another aspect of Walnut is its ability to put a shield or cloak of light around the aura to give protection to those who feel and absorb the vibrations and impressions from all around them. This oversensitivity can make one withdraw from life and can often be felt in very negative or overcrowded environments. Negative energies are then drawn in through the auric field, usually via the solar plexus chakra, weakening and overpowering one's own energy.

When I first started working as a practitioner, I found that I was picking up the energy of each client and still hanging on to it when with the next person, therefore unable to give my full attention and focus to the Now. I started taking a few drops of Walnut in a glass of water, sipping it throughout the day. I soon found that I was fully present and the essence was acting as a link breaker, freeing me from the old to go onto the new. Unlike Honeysuckle, where the negative personality is more consciously living in the past, feeling sadness and regret; Walnut is far more subtle in its workings and is more for when one is unconsciously linked to the past on the astral planes. Walnut is for when one is confronted by change of any kind, or when one feels overpowered by the energy of others, unable to focus on one's own path and ideas. As the Walnut is taken so the subtle bodies become stronger and are no longer so easily influenced by others. Thus Walnut is for transition, change and protection.

Water Violet *Hottonia Palustris*

WATER VIOLET

POSITIVE QUALITIES

- Open heart chakra. Able to share love with others.
- Knowing all are equal. Wise, tolerant, humble.
- Great inner dignity and serenity.

NEGATIVE QUALITIES

- Very aloof, proud and reserved with upright stance.
- Feelings of superiority, better than others.
- Loneliness due to barriers put up around heart chakra.
- Living in isolation. Needing to be alone.
- Independent, does not like interference. Spiritual pride
- Withdrawn, not able to show emotions.

Water Violet types are often old souls who carry much knowledge and wisdom. This personality can often have a 'special' Divine Mission, usually one of helping others, or working in a position of authority, using their great gifts for the benefit of mankind. When the personality is out of balance, the ego has taken the idea of 'specialness' and made it its own. The person then starts to feel they are far superior to others and develop much pride. They build a barrier around the heart so that they are not able to link into others, in an energetic sense, bringing feelings of loneliness. This effectively closes down the heart chakra which should be open, loving and sharing, and blocks the flow of Divine Love from the Universe to self and from self to others. People sense this barrier as a coldness and the individual seems unapproachable. In this way the isolation felt by the mind is reinforced by the reality one creates with these thought patterns. The person in this negative state will often say they are happy on their own, due to their independent nature, and will not admit to anything else. As the flower essence of Water Violet is taken so the personality feels more connection with Source, and thus with others, thereby creating the new reality where others feel they can communicate with one. The barriers start to dissolve as one comes to the humbling recognition of the truth of the oneness of all people. When in this positive state, as the heart chakra opens up, these wise old souls are sought out by others for their wisdom and guidance. These people often make excellent teachers and counsellors, able to share from the depths of their experience.

Water Violet types can often be identified by their straight, upright backs and stance, symbolised by the beautiful pale lilac flowers which reach out of the depths of the water (the emotions) on tall upright stems reaching for the sky (the spiritual realms). When needing this essence, one can develop knee problems, as these joints are symbolic of kneeling in prayer and humility. Those on a path of self knowledge will sometimes need this flower essence as they can often develop spiritual pride.

White Chestnut *Aesculus Hippocastanum*

WHITE CHESTNUT

POSITIVE QUALITIES

- Calm, peaceful mind
- Goes to sleep easily.
- Able to think positively and clearly.
- Able to focus mind on one thing, more organised.
- Easier to meditate.

NEGATIVE QUALITIES

- Mind confused, unable to focus on one thing.
- Too many thoughts, strong mental activity.
- One thought going round and around in one's mind.
- Feels like hamster on a wheel.
- Restless sleep.
- Unable to concentrate.
- Mental arguments and conversations.
- Unable to switch mind off to meditate, etc.

White Chestnut is needed when the mind is unable to "switch off". Often we are bombarded with ideas and talk from others and can tend to reach overload; the mind can then become confused, unable to process so much information at once and our thoughts go round and around like a caged hamster on a wheel. We find we are unable to switch off this mental clutter to gain peace of mind. This process can happen by watching too much television or hearing excessive radio when our soul needs peace which can more easily be obtained in silence. In this silence, deep within our heart we can hear our intuition/guidance and receive deep healing through meditation or prayer.

Our mind may be occupied by thoughts of the day, the past, future or even a song which goes on continually in our mind and we cannot get it out of our head. At other times our workload is heavy with, seemingly, too many things to do and we are unable to focus on one thing. Maybe we have thoughts of a conversation or argument we had and cannot get it out of our mind, continually re-running it in our head to see how it could have been different. Any of these patterns of too much mental activity can create headaches and much tension in the head. As the White Chestnut is taken the mind is able to relax and focus on one thing without distraction.

Wild Oat *Bromus Ramosus*

WILD OAT

POSITIVE QUALITIES

- Knowing ones Divine Path.
- A sense of purpose.
- Direction in life is clear.
- Good at many things.

NEGATIVE QUALITIES

- Lack of direction in life.
- Unsure at times of change.
- Never found the right occupation.
- Frustration/lack of fulfilment.

One would take Wild Oat flower essence when needing to see the way to go forward. This is not just for career moves but also for times when wishing to see ones true path. Maybe you are unsure about a marriage, relationship, whether to have a family or travel. We each have a Divine Path, the direction our Soul wishes us to gravitate towards. This sense of purpose can be found deep within us, when we instinctively know that our direction is right. We each have a different path of growth, aspects we have developed in previous lives we incarnate to "shine" in, or work we have chosen to come to earth to do, to develop our soul, in Divine service to mankind. It is only through this path we find true fulfilment otherwise we feel lost and aimlessly move through life, from job to job never finding happiness.

If you have never found fulfilment in life or in work and you have had a great succession of unsuccessful or boring occupations, you need to take this essence.

When we follow the dictates of our soul we start to enjoy life to the full.

The tall Wild Oat plant hangs its head among the hedgerows and bends to point the way forward. I can imagine Dr. Edward Bach saying "the thing that makes us most happy is what we came here to do!"

Wild Rose *Rosa Canina*

WILD ROSE

POSITIVE QUALITIES

- Enthusiasm for life.
- Does not put off tasks.
- Accomplishes things easily and effortlessly.

NEGATIVE QUALITIES

- Dull and lifeless.
- No enthusiasm.
- Apathetic, cannot be bothered.
- Puts tasks off for another time.

Wild Rose flower essence is needed at those times when one feels unable to enthuse about life, unable to accomplish tasks due to sluggishness and apathy, when we continually postpone doing something until later but later never comes.

The person in this negative state can often be identified by a dull, monotone voice which drones on with no highs or lows, their speech reflects their boredom with life.

My own experience with Wild Rose was this. Having moved to a new house there were problems with the drains and although I knew what to do to fix it, I kept putting it off as I did not relish the thought of rectifying it. After six months I still had not completed the task. One day I was thinking which of the essences I had rarely taken, wishing to have the experience of all the flower essences. I realised I had never taken Wild Rose (it is not my usual characteristic!), and so promptly put a couple of drops on my tongue. Within half an hour I had driven to the tool hire company, hired a set of drain rods and in an hour or two had successfully completed the task. I have never been guided to take Wild Rose again as I have not needed it.

Most people experiencing the negative state of this flower would need to take it over a period of time; my sensitivity is very heightened when working with the essences, which is why I only needed one dose, also, it was not a deep rooted state.

Willow *Salix Vitellina*

WILLOW

POSITIVE QUALITIES

- Loving gratitude for all.
- A forgiving nature.
- Holds no grudges.
- Knows one is treated fairly and always gets exactly what one deserves.

NEGATIVE QUALITIES

- Resentful and bitter.
- Cynical nature.
- Feels unfairly treated.
- Finds it difficult to forgive.
- Bears grudges.

The Willow flower essence is the one that brings the energy of forgiveness. Willow helps us come to the understanding of the Universal Laws, particularly the law of cause and effect. With the understanding of past incarnations which we all experience to enable our Souls growth as it participates at a physical level in all emotions and mental patterns; so we know that we have alternately misused power, possibly abused others and have also chosen to be abused. Whether it be mental torture or physical or any other "perceived" injustice it is simply Gods way of giving us a golden opportunity for forgiveness. How else would we learn it? When we forgive others we give them a blessing and we also receive a blessing, for we only gain by giving to others with an open heart. Maybe we caused harm to the other person in a past life giving them the opportunity to grow and find their own power. Maybe this person is one you have a soul link with and you agreed, before birth, to meet up together so you may have these experiences. As you forgive and bless the other, with an open heart, knowing their anger, fear etc. are simply expressions of the ego (lower self) so you are helping the other to grow, for your love will dissolve any guilt within them and help them to be more an expression of their true or higher spiritual self. Forgiveness does not mean we have to tolerate deep injustices or be weak in our nature. Forgiveness comes from a loving heart which can also be strong and powerful in its expression. As we release anger, grudges and bitter feelings to others (and this includes all you have ever had experiences other than love with, including family and close relationships) so we are releasing them from our incorrect judgement i.e. that they have in some way harmed us. In this release you have the experience of growing and opening your heart further and most importantly you feel better. Do it, if you wish for this reason only, as long held bitterness and resentment can create havoc in the physical body, causing rigidity and pain. A loving face is one of beauty whatever its age or features. For more help with love and forgiveness try reading "The Course in Miracles" or "A Return to Love" by Marriane Williamson or "Love is Letting Go of Fear" by Gerry Jampolski.

Clockwise: Cherry Plum, Clematis, Impatiens, Rock Rose, Star of Bethlehem

EMERGENCY ESSENCE

Emergency Essence is a combination of 5 different essences. These are Star of Bethlehem, Impatiens, Cherry Plum, Rock Rose and Clematis.

Collectively these essences work on releasing shock, trauma, upsets, tension, panic and helps one stay grounded and conscious. A very powerful combination which can be used at any time one feels the need to be calm and balanced, or in any emergency situation:

- Before driving tests, exams, job interviews etc. to stay calm and centred.
- When one hears bad news or is emotionally upset, bereavement, grief etc.
- Before a hospital or dentist visit and before and after operations.
- When accidents happen Emergency Essence speeds up the healing process and keeps everyone calm.
- Sudden shocks, knocks, burns, sprained ankles etc.
- Stressful situations at work.
- For fear of flying, before and while travelling.
- If someone faints or loses consciousness, put it on the tongue or rub on lips, wrists, pulse spots. They will revive quickly.
- For the mother whilst in labour and giving birth (also to the new-born baby, pulse points).

4 drops can be taken on the tongue or in a drink to be sipped and this can be repeated as often as is needed in any situation.

Here are some times when I have found the Emergency combination extremely valuable:

When I took my driving test I was quite nervous, so I took it in all my drinks the day before and on the test day several times on my tongue. I arrived at the test centre very calm and passed easily.

On sprained ankles, pulled muscles, etc., I have often put the essence directly onto the skin (as long as the skin is not broken) and rubbed it in. I find that often there is not a bruise the next day and the pain goes almost straight away. Do this as often as necessary, you may also put 6 drops in a small cup of water to swab on any area of pain or discomfort.

I, fortunately, do not suffer from nerves when at the dentist, but many find it invaluable then. I have found it a great help to quickly release the effects of a dentists injection and to heal the mouth and gums.

In car accidents, Emergency Essence has proved to be a life-saver. One must, of course, also phone for an ambulance in these situations, but however bad the accident seems, the essence will help release the shock which gets locked in the body, blocking the self-healing process, so that any injury will be healed very quickly.

Once in Spain, driving along, Jeremy and I came to a sharp bend where an accident had taken place. The man whose little Fiat had just collided head on with a Landrover, was staggering across the road, red in the face, clutching his heart in the throes of a heart attack. We jumped out and I ran over with the Emergency Essence from the car and gave him a few drops on his tongue, twice. Within a couple of minutes he was back to normal and calmly sat down. We then sent him some healing and he got up and walked back to his car to examine the damage!

I have given clients a bottle of Emergency Essence when they have been going to hospital for operations. Each time, everything has gone smoothly and, when taken before and after, there has been rapid recovery to the doctor's amazement, with no side effects or sickness when regaining consciousness.

Emergency Essence then is an invaluable first aid tool for the handbag or car. If you carry a bottle with you it will help in all sorts of situations. Not just for accidents or trauma, but to help balance the emotions or recover from bad news. It is also very helpful for bereavement situations to heal grief and shock.

In my healing workshops there is always a bottle available, as often in healing work emotions and pain are released which have been suppressed or held onto for a long time. The wonderful healing energies quickly bring it to the surface for clearing and the essence bottle is invaluable. A great tool for any therapist or healer to keep in their practise room.

Emergency Essence is also available in organic cream form with the addition of Crab Apple, Pine and Arnica to heal the skin. I have had great results on clients with the cream for skin problems like acne, eczema and psoriasis. It is also wonderful for damaged skin, cuts and burns etc. which heal rapidly.

HOMEOPATHIC POTENCIES

The flower essences in this book are not Homeopathic potencies. It is important to understand that the original writings and teachings of Dr. Edward Bach did not INCLUDE MAKING STOCK BOTTLE TINCTURES IN HOMEOPATHIC POTENCY. The wonderful idea behind his original work was the simplicity of the system, the fact that anyone could buy a set of the essences and prescribe them for others without too much knowledge and without lengthy homeopathic training. This original process is STILL continued by Heartsong in the making of mother tinctures and stock bottles – two drops being taken from mother tincture to prepare a stock bottle. The stock bottles on sale to public which can be further diluted are loosely based on homeopathic principles BUT IT IS NOT HOMEOPATHY. This original method does not involve succussion, (a form of dilution and shaking), and therefore could not be claimed to be a 4x homeopathic potency. If this potency is claimed on a stock bottle – MAYBE IT HAS BEEN SUCCUSSED AND THEREFORE NOT PREPARED ACCORDING TO DR. EDWARD BACH'S ORIGINAL WORK – BE AWARE OF THIS!

The simplicity of the system Edward Bach discovered lies in the fact that 2 drops of stock level essence can be further diluted to make up to 30 ml. of a medicine or dosage strength. From this, 4 drops can be taken from 4-10 times a day as is necessary. While the essences taken at this level work very quickly on transient states of mind and emotions, they need to be taken over much longer periods of time to effect change at very deep emotional and mental levels. Until now, if one was suffering from very deep rooted negative states the essences would need to be taken over a period of months or sometimes years to bring a transformation into the positive state, especially in deep states developed in childhood or held in the subconscious mind from past incarnations or other dimensions of self.

I personally have taken many of the essences over long periods, to transform my personality level. Gradually, the changes come until the essence is no longer needed and the positive aspect is permanently in position. Even then there may be the occasional lapse into the negative state but by that time the consciousness has changed so much that it is immediately recognised and shifted by a positive thought or just 1 or 2 doses of the essence. However, as we move fully into the new 2000 year cycle, the Golden Age of Aquarius with all it relates to, rising consciousness and spirituality, healing etc., many people seem to feel the essences speeding up their process. We are being urged by our spirit, souls and the Ascended Masters on the other dimensions to wake up quickly and many rays of healing energy are being directed to this planet from the Universe to help us with humanity's spiritual awakening and healing, many of which it has been my joy to anchor as part of the Eternal Light® Healing System. As our consciousness raises so we become aware that we are not isolated, individualised units of consciousness but are all ONE and linked subconsciously through the dimensions.

Therefore, what happens to one individual will affect not just those around, family, friends, etc., but ultimately every other member of our earthly family. Just as the barriers of countries have broken down, Russia, Germany, Europe etc., so our individual barriers are being demolished by visions of oneness. Some start to recognise that if we are cruel to others so that energy is reflected back to us and we receive the same in return. "AS YE SOW SO SHALL YE REAP" said Jesus. Others are affected by our energy field on all dimensions, some subtle, some more concrete. As we recognise the need to change ourselves more urgently, knowing our inner changes and outer responses will also help to heal others and the planet indirectly, so the need for higher frequencies of vibrational medicine are needed. This is why myself and many other people have been guided to develop further flower essences at this time to help with the accelerated growth of all humanity.

The time to use the other gem and flower essences is when you have been working on a particular aspect of your personality for a long time. Maybe you have taken Mimulus to transform known fears or Centaury to become less subservient. Over a period you have felt changes in these aspects but still feel stuck at some level. At this time there are two ways to go forward, assuming your original choice of essence was correct, either look at the group of essences covering the Mimulus (FEAR group) or Centaury (OVERSENSITIVITY) and read the chapter on Karmic essences. If it feels right or you may meditate on the subject or dowse, take the appropriate Karmic essence (Pink Rose or White Bluebell in the case of Mimulus or Centaury) until the last of the negative aspects are released, or take the appropriate combination essence or shift the blockage with one or all three of the Bach Star of Bethlehem, Wild Oat or Holly catalyst remedies.

KARMIC FLOWERS

This group of powerful healing flower essences have been given to the world, from Divine Source, to help facilitate a deeper healing process within us at this time. Seven of these essences cover each of the seven groups that Dr Edward Bach placed his flower essences in. These seven categories are discussed in this book. Much information has been channelled from other dimensions since Edward Bach's physical death on flower and gem essences, and the importance of this work for the new Golden Age we are entering cannot be over emphasised. We know now, through this extension work that each flower, gem, crystal, and mineral has its own vibrational frequency to help mankind in some way.

The information given by the Ascended Masters in the other realms is that Edward Bach's wonderful original discovery of 38 essences, a complete whole in itself, is working to treat, transmute and balance states of mind developed in this lifetime, i.e. womb onwards.

Psychologists are aware that as a baby in the womb we are susceptible to all states of mind and emotions of the mother which are then imprinted in the consciousness of the child to later manifest when born. This can now be monitored by new scientific equipment. The baby can be seen relaxed and peaceful when gentle music is playing or the mother is meditating. More disturbingly, the child in the womb can be seen to be in great discomfort when the mother is angry, upset or in pain.

The importance of treating expectant mothers with flower essences is therefore obvious, as it has a knock on effect on the baby. Likewise, after birth the essences taken by the mother are passed onto the child through the breast milk. Essences can also be given direct to the baby, dabbed on nipples or if bottle fed, put in the bottle itself. Helping the baby in this way will stabilise the child and give him or her a great start in life.

Star of Bethlehem is good given to all babies immediately when born and also the mother while in labour and just after. This will help to release the shock of coming into a physical incarnation from the comparative safety and peace of the womb, and before that spirit. The mother will have less pain and a much easier process.

Emergency essence which has Star of Bethlehem in the combination would be as good, if not better in the above situation. It can also be diluted in water and swabbed over the mothers face and stomach during labour.

In addition to the thoughts and patterns of the mother, picked up by the child in the womb, we also carry subconscious patterns into this lifetime which then form our own individual consciousness for this incarnation. These patterns or energetic frequencies can mean the difference between a peaceful, calm mind and therefore life, or a fearful and angry one. These patterns are not manifested randomly, rather they are chosen by the soul and guiding Ascended Master before birth so that certain patterns which have not been transmuted in past lives or different dimensions, may be worked with and cleared in this life.

Our main purpose on the Earth is to learn about unconditional love and to manifest that frequency and on this planet we have chosen to learn through duality, (polarity consciousness); therefore through fear, anger, pain, guilt, etc. Through all of these experiences our soul can grow and develop in all areas chosen. When all lessons have been worked through and thoroughly learnt, (when we have become totally heart centred and unconditionally loving), we may then chose to end our cycle of incarnations on the earth and go to other dimensions, planets or star systems for different kinds of growth in further incarnations there.

Remember, we are all eternal beings who exist multi-dimensionally. Stuck inside our physical bodies, looking at the world through 3D eyes, it is very difficult sometimes to see that there is a higher purpose to all of this.

The karmic flower essences help release and clear very deep rooted states of mind from the subconscious. These thought patterns are deep within us and form our core belief structure. We all have bottom line thoughts which affect our conscious mind and life process.

All of these underlying imprints affect our everyday life, although we are usually quite unaware of this, until we start to heal our thoughts and personality, often through illness as the activator (its only purpose!). These negative core beliefs are carried into our subconscious in this life as past life memories, patterns from parallel dimensions, according to your understandings or inner knowing.

Added to this heavy package of negativity are the ideas, attitudes and consciousness of the society structure that we are born into and all those energies from previous civilisations which may still be influencing us and are held as thought form structures around the astral levels of this planet.

All thoughts carry consciousness or energy. As an example the fears, horror, guilt and anger from the second world war have been energetically carried since that time as bands or clouds of negative energy, directly over Europe, Japan, and other areas. These bands of energy then continue to influence the thoughts of those on earth until they are cleared away by positive energy or light. Each time we get angry or fearful we are not just feeling our own thoughts and therefore emotions, but we are tapping into that huge thought form in the atmosphere and it is feeding our own patterns. Likewise each time we experience a negative thought we are adding to the huge databank in the sky.

To understand how this happens we need to have an understanding of Universal Law, particularly the Law of Attraction, commonly known as like attracts like. All thoughts are energy and can create. They create emotions, which are energy in motion. Thoughts can create positivity or negativity. We send these thoughts as energy from our minds into the aura, and these can be clearly seen clairvoyantly as colours or moving energies, with each thought having its own frequency. Thus our energy field is made up of these patterns. The Law of Attraction ensures that we attract to ourselves only those in tune with our frequency, or those needing that energy for a particular lesson, purpose, or healing. Likewise, as we tune into others in this way so we link into other energies or mass consciousness surrounding Mother Earth with each feeding the other. Thus, the only way out of our individual, human and earthly dross is by each one of us consciously changing patterns. As we do this, we clear not just from ourselves but from the All. As this is happening now on a world-wide scale so the light energies have now become stronger than the dark.

This is ensuring the survival of humanity and Mother Earth, for until quite recently we were heading for destruction. This has now changed. The consciousness of humanity, and therefore Mother Earth (we are all one) is rising very quickly. One of the Ascended Masters whom I channel, Kuthumi, says that we are changing so rapidly now that any plans made by the higher, light, guiding forces of the planet, the White Brotherhood, often become quickly outdated because of our conscious growth. They are so pleased and excited that the earth will once again become a clear and pure positive place to be in, a paradise in fact, as it was in the beginning of our time. As we all consciously become clear, so we open up to higher levels of consciousness or thought and recognise not just our own divinity, but the interconnectedness of all life forms on the planet. New ways of living, of industry, commerce, agriculture etc. will come about as a result of our changes. These will be based on unconditional love rather than greed, power or control.

This is our destiny, choose to be part of this change and transformation, and join in the excitement which so many of us are now feeling for the future.

It is important to have these understandings, to know the relevance of flower or gem essences for healing and inner growth, particularly to release old karmic patterns fast!

Pink Rose

FEAR AND ANXIETY GROUP

PINK ROSE

If you have ever taken any of the fear group of essences from the 38 consistently over a long period of time and you know they have worked to some extent but you feel that you have reached a plateaux, now would be a good time to take Pink Rose. This essence releases deep rooted states of fear from any source other than those generated in this lifetime.

I myself have released a lot of trauma with this essence. As I am very sensitive, just a few drops on my tongue, when guided, has brought to my conscious mind and cleared a couple of Atlantean lives and powerful second world war concentration camp trauma. I had taken Cherry Plum occasionally, when needed for some years, before taking the Pink Rose and clearing the Auschwitz life fears. Incidentally as I was releasing the emotional pain and seeing what happened during that lifetime, I suddenly remembered that when I was 12 years old, while other children were reading Enid Blyton, I went to the adult section of the library and read as many books as I could find on German concentration camps. These were subconscious memories that were coming to the surface for that trauma to be finally cleared. Since that powerful clearing I have not needed Cherry Plum again, that fear has been released, transmuted and cleared away.

WHEN TO USE?

- Phobias or fears unrelated to this life.
- Fears held since birth.
- Very deep rooted fear.
- During healing or past life regression.
- Deep fears remembered in dreams/nightmares.

White Bluebell

OVER SENSITIVITY GROUP

WHITE BLUEBELLS

For those who have always been over-sensitive since childhood, often feeling hurt or sensing very strongly other people's emotions and thought patterns. Many working in the healing arts are susceptible to these patterns and end up closing themselves down as life becomes too difficult when processing others' "stuff" or having one's own emotions triggered. This is of course so that these energy patterns can be cleared; knowing that however, does not always make it easier. I have found that most sensitive people have a wide open Solar Plexus chakra, which is tuning into others thoughts and emotions on a lower psychic level, (the higher level being the brow chakra). It is mainly at the Solar Plexus that we tie or cord into others, subconsciously, and they also tie into us. These energetic frequencies can be seen clairvoyantly and it simply means that we give and take energy to and from each other. This is not healthy, as we all need to be in our own space with our energies intact, not being drained by others. When we are so over influenced by others we give our own power away and do not develop our own individuality. As the White Bluebell is taken, so this over-sensitivity is balanced. We need the sensitivity to help us in our work or area of life that we chose this energy for; to empathise with others, use psychic skills etc., but like all energies, we need it to function in a balanced way to achieve our ultimate purpose. Many people develop fears due to their over-sensitive nature, they can be easily hurt or upset by others or situations. Try a course of Walnut essence first; this may be enough to balance you.

The effect of White Bluebells is usually felt very quickly and much relief is obtained, energy levels rise and the aura is strengthened.

WHEN TO USE?

- If picking up others emotions and pain, feeling it.
- Solar Plexus over-sensitive.
- If you need to put hand over Solar Plexus in crowds to protect yourself.
- Needing protection from the energies of others.
- Please also see Walnut.

Wild Iris

OVERCARE AND CONCERN FOR OTHERS

WILD IRIS

When our concern for others becomes so strong and feels very deep rooted, or, as with all of these karmic essences, locked in at some level, Wild Iris will help to release these worries.

Often in the past we have been involved in positions of authority and have developed feelings of responsibility for others. Overcare for others is also a powerful but subtle form of control. If you look at the essences in this group one can see the need to control others through the desire to be in charge, as in Chicory and Vine, or through criticism, Beech.

I have always had deep feelings of responsibility for the planet and the spiritual development of humanity. Now with full conscious recollection of the past, I am able to relate this to an incarnation at the fall of Atlantis when my chosen path was to uphold the light to keep the balance between the ego states of power and control which were rapidly taking that civilisation over. Many of us entrusted with that task have since felt a deep sense of responsibility for the future of Mother Earth and its inhabitants and a great sense of failure. Many of us knew we could no longer help the situation so 20 years before the continent went down; we took our groups to various other places, including Egypt where we started new pure civilisations. Since taking Wild Iris I and many others have cleared these deep subconscious memories and now feel much lighter, knowing that this time around we cannot fail our Divine Mission, and that Atlantis was simply part of our learning to understand the destruction caused by the misuse of Will.

WHEN TO USE?

- Feeling of deep responsibility.
- If you sense a misuse of power in the past.
- Feeling of huge karmic burdens.
- When the need to be in control or to change others is extremely deep-rooted.
- Always feeling a weight on ones shoulders.
- Feelings of a failure to hold enough light.

Wild Orchid

UNCERTAINTY

WILD ORCHID

Uncertainty originates from a feeling of separateness from our Source, of that part of us which has a full understanding and knowing of all things. When we are connected with this Divine Truth within us (a paradox, as we tend to think of our spirit or soul as something outside of us and this thought has to change,) we always know the right thing to do instinctively. With this intuitive inner knowing that we are connected and are a part of God or the creative source, indecision changes to decisive thoughts and actions, hence we become co-creators with God, using our minds and bodies to create and heal. As we learn to trust and follow our guidance, (Divine Will), so our path flows with the energy of the universe and not against it. We can then be guided to all sorts of wonderful experiences and new opportunities. As Wild Orchid is taken it raises our consciousness, leaving behind the negative vibrations of uncertainty as these thought patterns cannot exist in the new higher vibratory frequency.

Wild Orchid is an important flower essence for those that have taken much Cerato or Scleranthus from the uncertainty group but for whom there still appears to be deep imbalance in this area.

Meditating in a field of Wild Purple Orchid has the same effect temporarily; however, a more permanent heightened awareness can come about from the ingestion of the flower essence.

WHEN TO USE?

- When feelings of uncertainty are soul deep, after taking essences from the uncertainty group.
- When your inner knowing tells you your inability to act or decide is due to fears of repeating past mistakes, (take with Pink Rose).

Water Lily

LONELINESS

WATER LILY

The Karmic problem of this group is a loneliness brought into the consciousness of this lifetime by the soul, sending in a residue of memories from past incarnations when perhaps much time was spent alone or unable to communicate with one's fellow man. The difference between Water Lily and the existing essences in this group is that this loneliness will feel soul deep and bring with it an acute sadness, the depth of which is out of the reach of Heather, Impatiens or Water Violet.

I had been taking Water Violet for several months prior to the making of Water Lily, and to some extent my feelings of loneliness shifted. During a meditation I was given a strong feeling and shown where those patterns stemmed from. I was shown other lifetimes I had spent off the planet in other star systems and I felt a severe yearning to be back there, experiencing the unconditional love and peace of those times. Ultimately all those feelings and thoughts of not belonging anywhere on earth and patterns of separateness must be released so that we can be grounded, happy and committed to our mission here.

Many starseeds and lightworkers experience these emotions at some stage of their unfoldment. As we take the Water Lily the deepest aspects of our loneliness and sadness are gently eased away, bringing peace.

A customer wrote in to say that a client of hers had been seeking relief from some very distressing psoriasis all over his head and face, he had been everywhere and tried everything with no improvement. He was given a prescription of lotion for his head and cream for his face with Water Lily added as the vibrational frequency needed. His skin quickly cleared. When I went within to ask why he needed Water Lily instead of more obvious essences, I was told that he carried deep karmic loneliness from a past incarnation as a leper, ostracised from his village. As the pattern and loneliness lifted so did his physical manifestation of that deep memory. An unusual way to use the essences, but it worked.

WHEN TO USE?

- Deep heart chakra blocks and barriers.
- Wishing to return to past lives where you were in isolation, meditating in caves, etc.
- Soul deep feelings of isolation. See also Sweet Chestnut.

Valerian

DISINTEREST

VALERIAN

Valerian is the Karmic essence for a lack of interest in the present circumstances. Each of the flower essences in this group will give different indications of the states of mind that take one from the NOW. Often we are subconsciously locked into past incarnations, possibly to happier times in the soul memory to which it would like to escape, therefore we are unable to focus on the present. This personality type will have taken Honeysuckle from the existing range of essences and shifted much regretfulness. Another personality type may have needed much Clematis as their thought patterns tend to exist mainly in the future to what appears in day dreams to be better than the present. Again this state is relinquishing all power in the present moment in time, the only point of energy there is.

By escaping from our earthly commitment our Base Chakra becomes blocked with negative thought patterns and our hara does not function, (our will centre). We become very disorganised and unable to function well in the world, everything a muddle and disconnected. When we make a commitment to be here, now, fully present, we become a part of the living world and flow of life. We achieve far more in less time, easily and effortlessly, also feeling more at home in our bodies. Valerian is the key to unlock the door to the present, bring all the gifts and attainments from previous energy points, via the soul into the Now. Good for those needing continuous help to stay in their bodies.

WHEN TO USE?

- If you have always felt disconnected from your body.
- Permanent ungroundedness.
- Good for mediums, clairvoyants who get ungrounded easily.
- Base chakra closed
- Inability to function in life/the world.
- Please also see Clematis.

Yellow Rattle

DESPAIR AND DESPONDENCY

YELLOW RATTLE

Yellow Rattle is good for lifting out the remnants of despair at deep levels, after having been treated with any of the flower essences in this group for a period of time. When one is in the depths of despair unable to see any joy in life, Mustard, Sweet Chestnut etc. will raise one to a lighter level and bring relief. When, however, one is continually needing flower essences from this particular group, it is often a sign that this despondency is a frequency brought into this life to work with and clear by the soul energy. Underlying the depression is often fear as the bottom line core belief structure. It is necessary however to peel away the layers that we have built around ourselves in this life before we can start to work on clearing any deeper negative energies or "overlays" we have chosen to transmute. It is interesting that my clients would often describe the Cherry Plum fear state as depression and when one really knows these essences it is easy to see why. A client of mine who had been treated for a long time with Gorse and Mustard, on taking the Yellow Rattle, brought into consciousness the realisation that he had been in Auschwitz as a prisoner during WWII, in a past life. This insight was a catalyst for a final clearing of his deep depression. As can be seen, these essences work at very deep levels to clear core (causal) issues in a case.

Often the intense sadness carried by one in need of Yellow Rattle is not easy to describe. A melancholy which echoes from previous lives in a similar way to the dried seed pods in the flower. When winds cast upon a field of Yellow Rattle the sound will echo; the vibrations reverberating over surrounding fields in a similar way to the echoes of past hopelessness and despair. The essence dispels this deep seated energy.

WHEN TO USE?

- When reaching a blockage or plateau in the treatment of depression.
- When despair seems soul deep and untouchable with other essences from this group.

Lily

BRIDGING ESSENCES

Linking the seven Karmic essences to the original 38 flower essences are the trio of "spiritual light" essences I call the Trinity. These three flowers are like bridges of light linking the two systems together. Each person's vibrational requirements are different. Whereas some of you will have taken many essences from the original set of 38, over a period of time and may be ready to go straight into the Karmic healing, others may need one or more of the Trinity as a way of preparing for the deeper inner work of the Karmic seven. Others may never have taken any other essences but due to their vibratory frequency may be ready for the deep Karmic clearing. It is not a question of being good or evolved enough, it is simply that we all need different energies in our path at any given time, all is in divine order. DO NOT JUDGE!

LILY

The lily essence is for the spiritually insecure, bringing peace, serenity and comfort.

These souls are finally reaching their destination or lives purpose, bringing recognition of their true spiritual nature. This realisation can bring great feelings of insecurity and until they can actually become one with their spirit, they can easily have their faith and security shaken, sometimes rocking their very foundations.

This essence will bring back emotional and spiritual balance so that these souls can carry on, safe in the knowledge that God, Creator of all things, is guiding them and their foundations will, once again, become as solid as a rock.

I was given this description of the Lily essence, when, just after making it, I went to the Sacred Chapel of Saint Julian to pray. I asked to be given the function of the beautiful lily essence and St. Julian came through to me as a voice and I channelled a direct message, description above, which I immediately wrote down. After giving thanks, I returned home to see a client – which essence did she need? You guessed it, Lily! She was my first guinea-pig and after two weeks of taking it was feeling much more calm and secure.

Geranium

GERANIUM

For those in the dark and gloom, but recognising the need to contact their spirituality.

Like a person in a darkened room, moving around and bumping into things but unable to find the light switch. This is their essence. Their fingers will find the switch and their whole being will be flooded with light and love, which will in turn help to illuminate the world.

This essence is for those souls feeling the need to "wake up" or contact their spirituality, often for the first time in this life. They recognise that there must be something more, more than that which the material world has to offer. Sometimes this awakening comes after an illness or trauma of some kind, which then sends the personality searching for an inner reason or for deeper meaning to their life.

Each of us carries a light, deep within our hearts; a sacred space where there is eternal peace, joy and happiness. When we have built up many layers of doubt or fear in our lives it can be difficult to know or feel that place within us which carries Divine Love, Divine Wisdom and Divine Power. How do we start to experience it? Meditation is the only way to reach that centredness and inner calm. There are many forms of meditation and you will be drawn to the one that is right for you. To help you meditate at home, I have channelled a series of guided meditation CDs, so if you cannot find a local group to practice with or simply need some extra help you can listen to the CDs.

Using the essence made from this beautiful bright red flower can help to bring you closer to the inner sanctum of light, or at least the knowing of it, for in truth it is already there, a part of you as yet undiscovered but eternally waiting.

Fuschia

FUCHSIA

Helps to open up the heart chakra, bringing out that which has been locked inside. The floodgates will open, releasing any underlying pent-up emotions which cause blockages preventing spiritual attunement. Once these emotions have been recognised they can be treated and worked through, with any other essences. It is then that the person can recognise their karmic lessons, agreements and missions.

DOSAGE

While the Trinity may be taken for an average of four drops, four times a day as long as is necessary, it is important to observe stricter control with the Karmic seven. Due to their ability to release and transmute deep blockages try using the seven Karmic essences for three days only, four drops, four times a day. If you feel the pace of change within you is too fast, slow down to once or twice a day, or stop and try later. After three days, have a break from Karmic essences for seven days. This gives the opportunity for deeper issues to come to the surface to be released into the conscious mind and be cleared away. Sometimes it is important for our process to have this conscious knowledge or awareness of certain issues (often to give us the ability to help others with similar difficulties) before they can be transmuted. If this is the case it may be that what comes up for you needs an essence/s from the original 38 set to clear away patterns being brought to the surface. Usually I have found this to be one or more from the same group; i.e. if taking Pink Rose the Cherry Plum or Red Chestnut state might quickly come up and so make sure that you have access to a set or phone us for next day delivery. If unsure during this process help is on hand at the end of the telephone. If you phone Heartsong there are qualified, intuitive practitioners at hand ready to help prescribe and post the essences that you need. We are all Eternal Light® healers capable of sending distant healing if needed.

Sometimes the Karmic essence may appear not to have a noticeable effect, if so you may need to repeat the dosage for a further period of three days and continue the same process (three days on and seven days off) as long as is necessary. It can also be that the essence has cleared a very subtle pattern which is not very obvious on the surface. However, as with all essences, it is helpful to take exactly the right one at the right time, for good results.

Therapists, healers and those who have been working with flower essences for a long period may also intuitively choose an essence to take and may only need a few drops to bring an issue to the surface for clearance. I have found that this works for me and for very sensitive people. While meditating, if I have had pictures, karmic patterns or knowledge coming to me, I have come out of the meditation and taken the appropriate Karmic essence to clear the energies away, or taken it immediately afterwards.

Also, when I was practising I found them very useful during healing or past life regression work. Just a few drops put onto the clients tongue at the appropriate time can release so much. Any Karmic essence, especially Fuschia, can be helpful for stubborn blocks or resistance that you know is there within the client. These usages are supplementary, or used instead of the normal three days on and seven days off process. As with the diagnosis of all flower essences it is IMPORTANT TO DEVELOP AND USE INTUITION, INNER GUIDANCE OR DOWSING TO PRESCRIBE. The more that you trust this process the easier it becomes.

Due to the very high frequency of the Karmic and Trinity essences, the guidance from the Ascended Masters is not to dilute these 10. They lose up to 45% efficiency if diluted so use directly from the stock bottle unless your inner guidance tells you otherwise. The essences purchased from Heartsong are all stock level of potency, made directly from mother tinctures.

Often very little of the essence is needed to obtain quick results due to the swift effects and short dosage time.

DO NOT GIVE KARMIC ESSENCES TO CHILDREN. THEY USUALLY HAVE TO WORK WITH THEIR PATTERNS AS THEY GROW UP, SO IT COULD BE WRONG TO INTERFERE WITH THEIR KARMA. IT IS BEST TO JUST USE THE 38 ESSENCES ON CHILDREN.

INNER CHILD ESSENCES

Healing the Inner Child is one of the most empowering things we can do for our emotional well-being, which promotes a raising of consciousness, higher understandings of one's own childhood and, most importantly, a clearing of deep emotional hurts and imbalances. As we release fear, lack of self-worth, guilt and a myriad of other ego patterns, so we start to heal our inner child, that we may experience more joy, peace and love in our hearts and lives. This leads to a transformation of our life & more harmonious, loving relationships as we create a new reality.

This then brings deep emotional healing and transformation of the past to create a new future: one based on emotional and mental balance, restored inner peace, and, most importantly, more Unconditional Love. Resolving our unhealed issues helps to change our whole life for the better, including all our personal relationships. We then feel more joy and happiness, as our magical, healed inner child creates a more loving reality in our daily life, through our positive thoughts and emotions. This also helps to raise our consciousness to higher levels on our path of spiritual unfoldment, thereby healing us through all the dimensions of our being. Having worked on myself and clients with these beautiful combinations of flower/gem essences for over 20 years I have seen and felt their wonderful, transformational power.

Both the Inner Child Essences and related Inner Child Divination Cards are a joyful gift from the Ascended Realms, Mother Earth, and myself, that we may all become that Rainbow Warrior and Magical Inner Child that delights in helping to co-create a new Divine Future for all mankind.

HEALING THE INNER CHILD

The inner child is the small one, held within our hearts, who is often hurt or damaged in some way from incidents, shocks or trauma which often happened in childhood, but also later in life. Our very birth is often traumatic. Add to this the conditioning and attitudes of our parents, school teachers, the media and society generally, which we subconsciously adopt as our own. While some of these are positive attributes, many come from a negative ego perspective and can cloud the radiance of who we truly are. These lead to personality changes and emotional or mental patterns which then go on to affect our whole life and all relationships as the wounded child cries out for help and healing.

With a little introspection we can see how who we are now has been created from our past, and unless we can transform any negative patterns we carry, we will continue to create a future based on this past. As we create our own reality, based on the way we think, feel and act, we can start to see how we can change not just ourselves but all situations and relationships around us for the better. As we become clearer, the magical Inner Child is freed and our personality becomes lighter, more playful, creative and loving.

Healing the inner child is our biggest challenge in life! It develops a more positive personality, balanced emotions, more spiritual connection and the most powerful soul growth to be experienced in one lifetime. With higher levels of consciousness we know that there is no such thing as coincidence and we understand that we very purposefully chose the exact circumstances and family to be born into, before incarnation from the other dimensions, to best fulfil any karmic obligations and to give us the most perfect earthly vehicle for the growth of our soul. Many souls at this time have chosen to clear enormous amounts of karma to try to make this their last earthly incarnation and therefore seem to have had very difficult childhood's; however, the soul knew that at this very special time in Mother Earth's history all the help that was needed to become clear would be available to us. These Sacred Essences and the related Inner Child Cards are some of these tools of Light to help us transform and access more of the Unconditional Love, forgiveness, peace and joy held within us, so that we may then experience the incredible magnitude, power and abundance of our Highest Divine Being.

Developing ACCEPTANCE

- **Keynotes:** For self-denial, resentment, possibly 'victim-consciousness'.
- **Indications:** Feeling that life is unfair, or that one deserves much better. Unhappy with self and personal circumstances. Anger at the past or bitterness.
- **Positive qualities:** Loving understanding and acceptance of self, one's life experiences and relationships. True appreciation of one's unique gifts/potential.

Restoring BALANCE

- **Keynotes:** Can be universally applied for balance on all levels, especially emotional.
- **Indications:** Restless or oversensitive; mood swings, constantly up and down. Unbalanced emotions with an oversensitive Solar plexus and all that this entails. Too open to lower astral energies.
- **Positive qualities:** Complete balance of mind and emotions. Ability to integrate all life experiences. Self empowered. Able to create boundaries to give more space for self.

Fully Present to BE HERE NOW

- **Keynotes:** Can be universally applied for grounding.
- **Indications:** Spaced out, inattentive, unbalanced behaviour or lacking vital energy. May not hear what others say, possibly clumsy with many 'accidents'. Living in a dream world; unable to manifest ones Divine Mission in life.
- **Positive qualities:** Alert, fully present. More organised and focused. Has energy and enthusiasm to put one's dreams and ideals into practice, realising one's Divine Mission and full potential in life.

Releasing Trauma BIRTH

- **Keynotes:** Can be universally applied for releasing birth trauma. (Has also been applied to the new born child's feet and pulse points to great effect).
- **Indications:** Unwilling to be fully present. Patterns that relate to birth difficulties. *May also be indicated during major life changes/transitions*.
- **Positive qualities:** Secure and happy being here, no need to be constantly 'mothered'. Able to embrace change & transformation with ease and grace.

Restoring COURAGE

- **Keynotes:** Can be universally applied for releasing and clearing all fears, including karmic fear.
- **Indications:** Nervous or anxious. Subconscious fears and phobias inhibiting or ruling one's life. May feel cold all the time. Possible difficulties sleeping at night due to subconscious fears or nightmares.
- **Positive qualities:** Fearlessness. Challenges inspire one to act in a positive way, rather than re-act through fear. Courageous.

Becoming DECISIVE

- **Keynotes:** Blocked intuition. Lacking trust in one's own judgement.
- **Indications:** Too mental in approach to life. Inability to link up issues clearly to make decisions. Often fear of doing the 'wrong' thing due to past mistakes.
- **Positive qualities:** Decisive. Always trusting one's intuition, balanced judgement or inner guidance; uninfluenced by the choices/opinions of others.

Restoring DELIGHT

- **Keynotes:** Releases and transforms depression and an over-serious nature.
- **Indications:** Depression, gloom, possible resentment. Lacking spontaneity.
- **Positive qualities:** Joyful, positive nature, full of kindness, laughter and good humour.

Restoring Trust FAITH

- **Keynotes:** Lacking faith and trust that things will always work out for the best
- **Indications:** Sceptical, pessimistic or doubting nature, with an overly logical, questioning mind. Lack of trust often creates exactly the imagined 'negative', yet unwanted results within any situation, relationship or event.
- **Positive qualities:** Unshakeable trust and faith in life. Deep inner knowing that everything is in its right place and that we really do create what we project out into the world.

Patterns Related to FAMILY

- **Keynotes:** Helps to clear and release oppressive negative influences from inherited family patterns.
- **Indications:** Feeling a 'weight' or burden of 'family issues' overshadowing one.
- **Positive qualities:** Ability to feel more love towards one's family, yet freedom from any 'inherited' or unconscious patterns of the past.

Patterns Related to FATHER

- **Keynotes:** Father issues and/or problems relating to men. Male issues.
- **Indications:** Anger, difficulty or sadness over relationship with one's father and/or problems with masculine, more assertive side of one's nature. Possibly overly domineering, aggressive or insensitive.
- **Positive qualities:** More love, understanding and forgiveness towards one's father. Helps develop more balanced masculine energy within oneself. Comfortable with the more logical, assertive and male aspects of one's nature. Better relationships with men in general.

Developing FORGIVENESS

- **Keynotes:** Opens the heart to more love and forgiveness, also towards oneself.
- **Indications:** Easily bears grudges, hard-hearted or judgmental. Bitterness. May inwardly be in denial of any difficult relationships, to avoid facing inner feelings or suppressed anger.
- **Positive qualities:** Loving, forgiving, understanding and accepting nature. 'Lets go', doesn't 'hold on' to the past. Truly heart-centred.

Restoring FREEDOM

- **Keynotes:** Helps to release and clear controlling aspects of one's personality.
- **Indications:** Controlling or dominating behaviour. Rigid personality. May have an over-blown sense of self-importance. Always in the 'right'. Usually disinterest or fear of any situation where not playing a leading role.
- **Positive qualities:** Inner strength and self assurance. Seeing all as equals. Appreciates other people's unique gifts. Lets others learn and grow in their own way, without needing to 'help' or 'direct' them all the time.

Developing GOODWILL

- **Keynotes:** To release and transmute deep-rooted, recent or suppressed anger.
- **Indications:** Draws in confrontational situations (i.e. always meeting other 'angry' people) which then reinforces ill feeling or unconscious hostility towards others. May be in denial of inner feelings with lack of self-expression, creating many blockages at the Throat chakra.
- **Positive qualities:** Equanimity in all situations. Able to express oneself clearly in difficult situations or disagreements, in the moment, lovingly from the heart, honestly acknowledging any anger we may feel.

Developing GRATITUDE

- **Keynotes:** To transform any feelings of ungratefulness or resentment.
- **Indications:** Difficult to please. Appreciates little in life, usually taking life's gifts and others for granted. Resentful nature. Rarely says thank you.
- **Positive qualities:** Genuinely appreciative of everyone and all things in one's life. Expresses this appreciation and joy to all.

Transforming GRIEF

- **Keynotes:** For transmuting deep-rooted or recent grief and emotional loss.
- **Indications:** Deep feelings of sadness and loss, often after death of a loved one. Feels inconsolable and despondent. Emotional emptiness. Self pity.
- **Positive qualities:** More love and understanding of the transient nature of life and yet more awareness of the eternal nature of the soul and spirit. More joy as one realises and feels that, ultimately, one only grieves for one's own loss.

Attuning to GUARDIAN ANGEL

- **Keynotes:** Helps one to connect more with one's Guardian Angel, Higher Self and the Divine Realms.
- **Indications:** To forge a stronger link with one's spiritual path, spiritual self and soul for increased clarity and purpose in life. Helps develop more faith and understanding in the Angelic Realms that continually surround and support us.
- **Positive qualities:** Feels inspired and connected to one's higher self through gentle support, protection and guidance from one's Guardian Angel.

Restoring HUMILITY

- **Keynotes:** To transform inner or subconscious feelings of pride, superiority and separation from others.
- **Indications:** Too proud and aloof, finds it difficult to truly empathise and connect emotionally with others due to fears and barriers around the heart. Personal relationships that do not develop a truly loving expression.
- **Positive qualities:** Ability to fully integrate with and relate to others in a truly heart centred way, without fears of 'over-involvement', creating emotional cords, or losing one's own identity. Becoming more human.

Restoring INNOCENCE

- **Keynotes:** Transforms all feelings of guilt and uncleanliness.
- **Indications:** Self-dislike, self-disgust and all feelings of guilt and uncleanliness, especially over issues relating to sexual expression and intimacy.
- **Positive qualities:** Engenders feelings of purity, innocence and self-love. It becomes easier to have pure and innocent thoughts, and to forgive oneself, releasing any feelings of guilt.

Restoring INTIMACY

- **Keynotes:** Helps develop a warmer, more loving and affectionate nature. Transforms feelings of coldness and separation from others.
- **Indications:** Fear of relationships. Cannot express love and affection to those close in an informal or spontaneous way. Fears physical and emotional intimacy with others.
- **Positive qualities:** Affectionate, loving nature. No problem communicating and expressing these feelings in a spontaneous, demonstrative way – with a warm smile or a loving hug – appropriate to the situation.

Developing Divine LOVE

- **Keynotes:** To develop more Unconditional or Divine Love.
- **Indications:** Too hard-hearted or unloving, possibly due to past emotional hurts and wounds. Puts conditions on 'love' with many demands, cords and ties, or attachments.
- **Positive qualities:** Unconditionally Loving – without conditions.

Patterns Related to MOTHER

- **Keynotes:** Mother issues and/or problems relating to women. All female issues. Difficulties associated with sensitivity, intuition or creativity.
- **Indications:** Anger, difficulty or sadness over relationship with one's mother and/or problems with feminine or receptive side of one's own nature. Possibly oversensitive or emotionally needy. Problems with female issues.
- **Positive qualities:** More love, compassion or forgiveness towards one's mother. Helps develop the more nurturing, intuitive, feminine, sensitive and creative aspects of one's nature. Better relationships with women in general.

Connecting with MOTHER EARTH

- **Keynotes:** Ungroundedness through fears related to being here on Earth.
- **Indications:** Anxieties and fears often related to the wild, seemingly untameable and capricious aspects of Mother Nature. Constantly insecure as unconsciously perceives the whole world as a very unsafe place to be. Possibly spaced out, with many 'accidents'.
- **Positive qualities:** Feels confident and secure in all situations however alarming they may outwardly appear. Knows that all is in Divine Order. Enjoys being out in Mother Nature, feels very connected to Mother Earth. Fully present and grounded.

New Beginnings MOVING FORWARD

- **Keynotes:** For feelings of being stuck in a rut, unable to move on.
- **Indications:** Not knowing where to go or what to do next. Keeps repeating the same patterns or mistakes. Needs change, but unable to move out of the comfort of one's 'security zone' through fear or inertia.
- **Positive qualities:** Manifests one's visions. Enjoys change, takes new challenges in one's stride. Awareness and acceptance that one needs to fully work through any issue to avoid getting 'stuck' and repeating the same scenarios.

Transforming OBSESSIONS

- **Keynotes:** To transform obsessive or compulsive behaviour patterns.
- **Indications:** Focuses on one thing, to the exclusion of all else – cannot see a wider picture. Self-gratification or addictive behaviour that perpetuates itself as that part of one's consciousness gets stuck in the lower astral levels.
- **Positive qualities:** Healthy interest in many things, yet the ability to detach and let go – thus seeing their value within a wider, more inclusive perspective.

Releasing Trauma PEACE

- **Keynotes:** To gently release and transform all types of shock and trauma.
- **Indications:** Shadows cloud one's true radiance. Undermined confidence. Feeling numb or frozen inside, as if in a state of 'suspended animation'.
- **Positive qualities:** Unshakeable inner peace. Courage to look at and release any shock or trauma as it happens, and also from the past, rather than shutting down one's emotional responses through fear.

Developing PROSPERITY

- **Keynotes:** To transform 'poverty consciousness' into Divine Abundance.
- **Indications:** Feelings of lack and that there will 'never be enough'. However much one has, the lingering fear remains, consequently often hoards things, blocking the flow of abundance. These feelings of lack, of being undeserving, permeate all aspects of one's life affecting all relationships with others.
- **Positive qualities:** Divine Abundance flows in all aspects of one's life. Trust in the Universe to supply all one's needs when following one's Divine Path.

Feeling PROTECTED

- **Keynotes:** For over-sensitivity to the environment and energies of others.
- **Indications:** Feels vulnerable in crowded situations. Adversely affected by the emotional energies of others. Picks up too much on how others are feeling. Often becomes overwhelmed and drained of energy.
- **Positive qualities:** Balanced sensitivity. Can empathise with others without getting drained or corded in emotionally. Does not feel vulnerable in crowded, oppressive or discordant environments.

Transforming the way we RELATE

- **Keynotes:** Helps one communicate with others in a more open, honest way.
- **Indications:** Difficulty expressing one's true thoughts and feelings. Tendency to relate to others based on past preconceptions, or a need for approval. Suppressed anger or frustration through inability to express or be one's true self in the presence of others. May have colds, coughs or throat problems.
- **Positive qualities:** Is more one's true self, relating openly and honestly from the heart, in the now – without an overriding need to please, requiring approval or feeling nervous.

Cutting Ties RELEASE

- **Keynotes:** Helps to 'let go' of emotional cords, attachments and neediness.
- **Indications:** Cannot let go of people, situations or events. Emotionally insecure, requires attention or to feel needed. Can at times be very conditional or contrary. Over emotional, easily feels hurt and sorry for oneself.
- **Positive qualities:** Stands in one's own energy. More emotionally complete and balanced. Starts to feel and experience more Unconditional Love.

Developing SELF WORTH

- **Keynotes:** For loving and valuing ourselves Unconditionally.
- **Indications:** Self dislike, damaged self image or low self esteem. Feels unworthy, beats oneself up for not being 'good enough'. May strive to achieve or overwork to prove oneself and compensate for inner lack of self worth.
- **Positive qualities:** Values oneself, one's time, one's unique gifts and talents fully. No inner need to 'prove' one's worth or ability, to punish oneself or to compare oneself with others.

Restoring SIMPLICITY

- **Keynotes:** To transform an overly logical, left-brained and confused mind.
- **Indications:** Very mental in approach to life. Always complicates by trying to work everything out in a rational, logical, intellectual way. Blocked intuition; lacks faith and trust as finds it difficult to see things from a wider, more inclusive perspective.
- **Positive qualities:** Uncomplicated, balanced intuition. Life flows with ease as one develops greater ability to feel, trust, sense or simply 'know' what is right in any given situation, without having to 'work it all out'.

Integrating SOUL GIFTS

- **Keynotes:** Helps infuse more Divine Soul Qualities into one's daily life.
- **Indications:** Deep inner knowing that one has 'untapped' talents and creative gifts. May feel lacking in certain areas, at odds with one's inner feelings.
- **Positive qualities:** Enriches and inspires life through increased contact with one's Soul and Divine Abilities. Feels more joy and finds it easier to go within for guidance. Manifests one's creative and artistic inspiration.

Facilitating SOUL RETRIEVAL

- **Keynotes:** Helps re-integrate 'lost' aspects of one's personality that may have splintered off during times of shock, emotional stress and trauma.
- **Indications:** Incomplete or clouded personality. Damaged faith and trust in life. Often blind to, or has chosen to forget, issues related to past difficulties.
- **Positive qualities:** Feels more whole, joyful and more one's true self. Easily lets go of past fears/emotional pain as one re-integrates aspects of one's Soul.

Restoring STILLNESS

- **Keynotes:** Helps to release irritation and develop more patience.
- **Indications:** Impatient. May be easily irritated by the shortcomings of others. Fears there will never be enough 'time'. Inner tension, cannot switch off or slow down. May feel frustrated/suffer from nervous complaints.
- **Positive qualities:** Perfect patience/tolerance. Timeless nature. Gets things done, yet knows when to stop and always seems to have even more free time.

Restoring TRUTH

- **Keynotes:** Helps one express oneself clearly, from the heart.
- **Indications:** Withdrawn nature. Blocked throat chakra – cannot express feelings or emotions clearly. Often self conscious, may blush or stammer easily. May have much suppressed anger. May suffer from throat problems.
- **Positive qualities:** Can express oneself, one's emotional needs. Becomes more spontaneous, joyful and more of an expression of one's true self.

Restoring VISION

- **Keynotes:** Helps develop inner knowing, inner seeing and intuition. Helps one see the bigger picture. Releases fear of higher plane experiences.
- **Indications:** Very mental, gets stuck in details. Little vision in life short-sighted. Consciousness needs to expand to see beyond a purely material level.
- **Positive qualities:** More spiritualised inner knowing and intuition. Starts to see or understand the wider spiritual significance behind all creation. Knows one's Divine Purpose. Colours may appear brighter as clairvoyant vision is enhanced.

RAINBOW LIGHT BODY ESSENCES

These very powerful essences have been guided into being to help accelerate our process of accessing and attuning to our "light body". The light body is the very high frequency energy body, similar to the auric field, which can become part of us as our personality becomes clearer. Karma and old patterning is released through the use of flower and gem essences, healing, meditation or a few other therapies. As we release each fear, balance our emotions and learn to live in the now, trustingly and lovingly, with an open heart chakra; so our energy frequency and vibration rises higher and higher. Correspondingly the subtle bodies around us which form our auric field get cleared simultaneously with each release that we have. When the etheric, emotional and mental bodies have reached a very pure and clear level, we are able to manifest a fusion of the physical, ethereal and pure spiritual bodies forming what is known as the light body, higher self body or Mer-Ka-Ba.

In our subtle bodies are held all of the unbalanced emotions and fears, (emotional body), all our rigid thought patterns and attitudes, (mental body), and these very subtle energies affect us very directly. When these fields become clearer by using special breathing and healing processes (as taught on my Merkaba Meditation CD), so we can access higher frequency energies. These pure energies come from our spiritual connection to Source and from our soul. We are then able to access divine wisdom and truth from our brow chakra, acting in a loving way, unconditionally, from our open heart chakra; able to speak our truth from an open throat chakra and using our connection to integrate universal knowledge into our everyday life.

In this divine state of being, life is joyful and we are intuitively working as co-creators with Mother/Father God to achieve miracles on the earth plane. It is not the case, as some have thought, of ascending to other levels and leaving the earth. It is more bringing the 5th dimensional Christ consciousness down to the 3rd dimension; being it and living it. As we start to function in this way we become aware of how much more we can achieve through inner guidance, directed by our spirit rather than our ego. Working from spiritual guidance with chakras open and balanced is operating from a base of love, joy and compassion, whereas for thousands of years on the earth plane most people have functioned from the opposite, ruled by the ego and therefore coming from a place of fear, using power and greed as their motivating force. Soon, all individuals, governments, corporations and religions based on power and control will have to change or collapse as the energy of the earth and the majority of its inhabitants are rising vibrationally to become more loving, spiritually attuned and aware. The planet will no longer be able to accommodate the heavier, denser energies in her new light frequency.

In the interim period all darkness and karma is being drawn out of Mother

Earth to be released and transmuted; the war in the former Yugoslavia being a prime example.

In the spring of 1996, I led a team of seven dedicated healers to Croatia. We worked in refugee camps giving healing and natural remedies. The response was overwhelming; people who had nothing were so grateful for the healing and help that they received there were many tears of joy, the healers also experienced extreme growth. I donated three sets of 38 essences to two centres who organised our work and an allopathic medical doctor who had given up on orthodox medicine and was treating her patients with healing. When she came to the training course she said "You won't believe this but I've been praying to God for some natural medicine I could give to my patients to treat them more naturally!" The high point for me was to be able to initiate many people into healing energies and teach them the healing techniques, free of charge, so that they could spread the healing in the camps after we left. (For further adventures in the camps please read "Beyond Reiki Eternal Light®.")

I recently heard of another group who were still working in Croatia and sent them a donation of some 50 bottles of Emergency Essence to give away. People there told them that these are the same wonderful remedies that another lady brought to us some 20 years ago to help clear our war traumas!! How wonderful!

We recognised, while we were in Croatia, that different religious and ethnic groups can live together peacefully, as indeed they had before the war, and this was a situation caused by deep karmic patterns being played out and cleared. Part of the process of the raising of the earth's vibrations.

After the old ley line structures were cleared and purified, so a new 5th dimensional ley line grid system was put into place to help raise mankind's consciousness even more quickly.

The time is coming to open up all chakra (energy) points, cleansing and transmuting emotional and mental patterns blocking them, to radiate our true light. From other realms these can be seen clearly as colours forming a rainbow of light. This is the activation of the rainbow light body or Mer-Ka-Ba.

These light body essences were conceived from inner guidance and working with Ascended Masters and many Divine beings from Venus, Sirius and other star systems. Formations and mandalas of crystals, gem stones and minerals surrounded the under a pyramid stargate and sunlight for amplification, (except emotional body which was amplified under the full moon.) Many different rays of energy were sent through and information was received during this sacred process, which was shared by myself and Jeremy.

Since working with these essences and taking them myself I realise their inherent potential. They are very powerful and I recommend that you take one chosen essence just once a day. If you have not had any obvious blocks releasing after one week, try it twice a day. The best way is to follow your own inner guidance, you may be at a point where you can take two different essences once per day, never at the same time though, or near mealtimes. It is best to start very slowly. After an initial sampling I was guided to use Earth star in the morning and Hara later in the day. After two days I had pains in my foot, (activation of my Earth star for grounding me), and an ache in my spleen for ten minutes after taking the Hara, which only lasted for a few days but was important to release a block and connect the spleen to the Hara and Sacral chakra, all very powerful healing energies. I now feel more earthed and with the hara activated can actually accomplish more. The soul star at night was giving me powerful conscious dreams, working at a spiritual level. We all react differently to the essences as we carry different patterns. For example, when on the emotional body I experienced a lot of clearing, but Jeremy loved it and said it felt very nurturing, reawakening lost sensitivity. The mental body for him cleared a lot of stuck anger, though.

These essences have now been in use for the past 25 years by many people who have been drawn to them. I have had excellent results as have the many practitioners and others working with them. I also recognise that they are not for everyone. If reading this chapter makes you feel excited, then the essences are probably right for you, but as always, do follow your own intuition on selection.

As with all the essences in this book, they are offered as an opportunity for growth, as a gift from the heart of the universe.

EMOTIONAL BODY

Attuned to Archangel Gabriel

For fast clearance of imbalanced emotional patterns. The emotional body is the most difficult to clear of all the subtle bodies. E-motions are energy in motion, the energy created by our thoughts. Our emotional responses to others, life, and situations are 'learned' as a way of dealing with negative thought patterns behind the energy. This energy builds up and eventually becomes 'stuck' energy, blocking chakras and the subtle systems. This essence releases these deeply held blocks and fears stored in the emotional body, helping us to feel more balanced within. Our personal relationships with others will then become much more healing, open and positive.

MENTAL BODY

Attuned to Hilarion

For clearing the negative thought patterns and core beliefs held in the lower mental body subtle energy field. Each time we think, we create. Therefore, we need to be aware of this and become more responsible for our 'creations'. Releasing and transmuting negative deeply held thought patterns from the lower mental body help us to think more positively. Affirmations take a long time to transform thoughts.

This essence speeds up the process, allowing more access to spiritual thought and ideas from the higher mental body.

ETHERIC BODY

Attuned to Saint Germain

The blueprint for the physical body, therefore the clearer it becomes, the healthier the 3rd dimensional body. Energies filter through from other subtle bodies to affect this level, as do shock, trauma, drugs, alcohol, etc., with the effect that eventually holes and weak points appear in the aura. When these reach the etheric level and stabilise there, physical illness often follows. This essence releases and transmutes dense energies from the Etheric Body which have the potential to eventually manifest at a physical level. A revitalising etheric cleanse with the new vibrational frequencies of the 5th dimensional Violet Flame.

EARTH STAR

Attuned to Thoth

This subtle energy alignment point is about 9" below the feet in a direct line with the Base chakra and Hara. When the earth star is activated it brings alignment to Mother Earth, grounding us and giving us more focused energy. This also brings attunement to the earth's magnetic grid, giving us more balance and the ability to channel healing energies down for the earth's healing and channel energy up from the earth for our healing. The more grounded we become the higher we can go and attune to our multi-dimensional self, Ascended Masters, Heaven and the stars. AS ABOVE, SO BELOW.

SOUL STAR

Attuned to Lady Nada

This subtle alignment point is just above the higher chakras, over the crown. When open and fully functioning it is aligned with the soul, all higher energies, the stars and Universe. Therefore, more soul energy, guidance and healing can come through to the mind and body. It is often good to take this essence just before going to bed, as it activates dream recall and conscious remembrance of contact with guides and masters while sleeping or Divine guidance from one's Higher Self.

THYMUS

Attuned to Sananda

This essence helps to activate the thymus chakra which feeds energy to the thymus, which in most adults has become atrophied since childhood. The ancient, spiritually attuned civilisations all had this gland fully functioning as they recognised it's true purpose as the 'higher heart' centre or chakra point. When this chakra is fully opened we are able to feel Divine Love for all sentient beings and full compassionate energy. Activation of thymus chakra also strengthens the etheric blueprint of the immune system and stimulates all the associated feelings and senses of the higher heart chakra including unity consciousness.

HARA

Attuned to El Morya

The hara is a subtle energy centre just below the navel, (not the sacral chakra). This centre when fully activated brings through Divine Will in action and a true sense of purpose as well as feelings of fulfilment and a real sense of the pure energy of our physical body. We cannot complete our Divine Missions on the earth plane with this centre weak or inoperative. This essence helps to activate, clear and transform this energy point, as well as purifying and energising the spleen chakra so we may realise out limitless potential to fulfil our Divine Missions, using our creative gifts and power to fully manifest Heaven on Earth.

INTEGRATION

Attuned to Lao Tzu

This essence helps to integrate and balance the left/right brain activities which are connected to our masculine/feminine energies which also need balancing. While most of us over-emphasise one polarity, our right brain, (feminine, intuition, creative, etc.) needs to be functioning as an equal with our left brain, (masculine, logical, etc.) to create a balanced whole. This is vital for our blueprint of health and also for our further spiritual development on higher octaves on the spiral of evolution and consciousness. While most operate from mainly one polarity (usually the left brain) this needs to be functioning on equal terms with our right brain. Therefore this essence also helps activate our intuitive and creative gifts through integrating our masculine and feminine natures and stimulating all associated structures.

CRYSTALLINE RAY

Attuned to the Hathors

This essence will help to awaken the soul and cellular memory of the crystalline light body and bring these memories more into consciousness. When first incarnating on the earth our body was lighter in structure, containing keys and codes to our higher nature through crystalline energy which encoded our DNA and cells. This essence helps us to remember who we really are by activating the cellular memories of our original crystalline nature and the keys and codes to higher consciousness contained within.

MER-KA-BA

Attuned to Archangel Metatron

This essence is usually the last to be taken in the individual's rainbow light essence process, as all the other aspects need to be worked on first to enable this essence to activate and re-awaken the light body (or Mer-Ka-Ba) process. The Mer-Ka-Ba is the spiritualised auric field merging with the higher self, bringing the ability to dematerialise or teleport the physical body. This is the process used by advanced beings, Ascended Masters etc., and can only be activated by a fully open heart chakra manifesting pure unconditional love. The higher our consciousness, the more unconditionally loving and grounded we become. Following intuition rather than ego, the sooner we will merge a spiritualised auric field with our higher self. This enables us to radiate pure Unconditional Love and will help manifest the body of light known as the Mer-Ka-Ba. This essence helps trigger the cellular memory held deep within our consciousness.

I AM PRESENCE

Attuned to Sanat & Lady Venus Kumara

This essence helps to bring a more conscious connection to our I AM PRESENCE, or Higher Self, through which we can learn to hear, feel, see or know our Inner Guidance and Wisdom in a more profound way, as our Soul guides us in making choices for our Highest Divine Good, thus bringing us more lasting happiness, peace & joy. This Essence also helps us experience deeper, more profound meditation experiences, making it easier to slip into that deep space in meditation where we merge in Unity Consciousness & become ONE WITH MOTHER-FATHER GOD AND ALL CREATION.

CAUSAL BODY

Attuned to Helios & Vesta

Linking up with the Etheric, Emotional and Mental Bodies, a natural progression is the Causal Body Essence. Being one of the highest frequencies of all our subtle bodies, the Causal Body holds the 'BLUEPRINT' FOR OUR LIFE-PLAN on the higher levels, it is a receptacle, so to speak, for the consciousness of our soul, bringing with it all the issues we have chosen to experience in this life. Therefore it contains any previous incarnational energies or qualities needed to help, guide or be worked upon in this life time. This Essence brings in FEELINGS OF SECURITY and is a portal to higher consciousness through helping to integrate the memory pattern of the Causal Body into our being, and to bring this into alignment with all our subtle bodies. The guidance is that more people, because of the expansion in their hearts, are now able to utilise this Essence.

DUE TO THE HIGH VIBRATIONAL FREQUENCY OF THESE ESSENCES, PLEASE DO NOT GIVE TO CHILDREN.

ESSENCES FOR CLEARING AND BALANCING THE CHAKRAS

'Chakra' is a Sanskrit word meaning wheel or spinning disc of energy. Our physical body rejuvenates/energises itself not just with food and breath but also by receiving universal energy or 'prana' from the air around us. It does this by exchanging energy at the chakras or energy centres of the body through the auric field via the chakra points. Toxins, thought patterns, emotions etc., leave the physical body through the chakras. Chakras become blocked by long held negative states and pollution etc. which eventually can lead to physical disease.

There are seven main chakras, and many minor ones, which can be related to the physical organs, glands etc., also to colours, light and sound frequencies and different levels of consciousness. As our vibratory frequency rises due to our release of fears, unbalanced emotions and old patterns, so the chakras cast off energy blockages for transmutation.

The Chakra Essences are combinations of flower and gem or crystal essences, each of which is working on some aspect of the chakra it is related to. Physical difficulties are often created by unbalanced emotions or negative mental patterns, which, when unresolved can cause blockages in the flow of energy coming in and out of the related chakra and from there to the related glands or organs. Other energies can also block a chakra, reducing its ability to fully function. Pollution from the environment, especially in severe forms such as radiation toxicity, can create damage to the chakra subtle energy system, or there may be karmic reasons for blockages. All our old unbalanced emotions, rigid thought patterns or physical traumas stay locked within our energy field, incarnation after incarnation, until we are finally willing and able to release and balance this "stuck" energy from within our chakras and subtle bodies. Each is held within our cellular memory; deep within our tissues and cells is a resonance with all past fears, trauma, anger, ways of dying, etc. This helps us to keep alive somewhere deep within our consciousness the old issues we came to resolve and clear in this life. I will share a couple of examples of how these old energies can come through into this life and block the flow of energy into the chakras.

One lady came for a first level healing workshop and while I was using her to demonstrate healing on the couch, I saw clairvoyantly that she had a blocked sacral chakra. I did some healing there and showed the class how to clear the blockage. I sensed this blockage was related to a past life when she had been abused sexually and I also communicated with the spirit of a baby, still held within her aura and attached to her at the sacral chakra. I was then able to cut the ties and release the spirit to the right level of consciousness. I realised she'd had an abortion in this life and her guilt had kept the energy there until she released that thought pattern. Tears were shed during the session and afterwards I shared with her what I had tuned into. She realised she had been releasing her guilt with the tears and confirmed her abortion and that she had often felt unsafe sexually, although she knew that she had not been abused in this life. I advised her to take a bottle of Sacral Chakra essence, 4 times a day until the bottle was finished, knowing this would complete the healing through all the dimensions. She wrote me a letter saying that all her menstrual problems had cleared up and the lower back pain she had for years was gone. Needless to say she felt much better about her sexuality and safer with the opposite sex.

Another man, during a workshop, came up to me complaining of a sharp pain in his back. I could "see" on the other dimensions a knife protruding from his heart chakra at the back, an old death. This physical body, due to all his inner work, was now releasing, through the cellular memory, the physical pain of that death and the emotional pain of betrayal. I cleared the energy from the chakra and gave him some Heart Chakra combination to take. The pain went immediately but during the next few days he realised he had held a pattern of mistrust towards his brother and knew that this was related to his heart chakra and the physical pain he had felt. The combination essence brought this to the surface to be released, so that he could consciously work on forgiving his brother. Their relationship is much better now.

The chakra combination essences are wonderful tools for transformation, working on emotional, mental and spiritual dimensions to heal and transmute blocked energy. The combinations work on the subtle levels, in the auric field and through not just the chakras but the meridians and nadis. As our chakra system becomes clear, aligned and alive, so our energy field radiates colour, harmony and peace.

These gifts of flowers, gems and crystals, given to us by our Divine Mother Earth, help us towards balance and clarity so that we may be in a better position to fulfil our spiritual destiny on this dear planet.

The chakra essences are a wonderful tool for all kinds of healers, practitioners, acupuncturists, reflexologists, etc., as they are so easy to diagnose and treat. These combination essences may be used however by anyone wishing to heal themselves or others.

Here is a list of the essences and a few of the issues they may be addressing. It was a great joy to spend time in NZ working with the beautiful land of ancient Lemuria, the devas and spirits of the special unique plants and trees. I was joined at one time by a group of Whaitaha "grandmothers" from the higher dimensions who explained to me how they had used these plants in the past. This was a very special and sacred experience for me. The Whaitaha were the very spiritual tribes who first inhabited Aotearoa (land of the long white cloud).

These combinations are now made by Aotearoa Essences in New Zealand and are stocked by Heartsong.

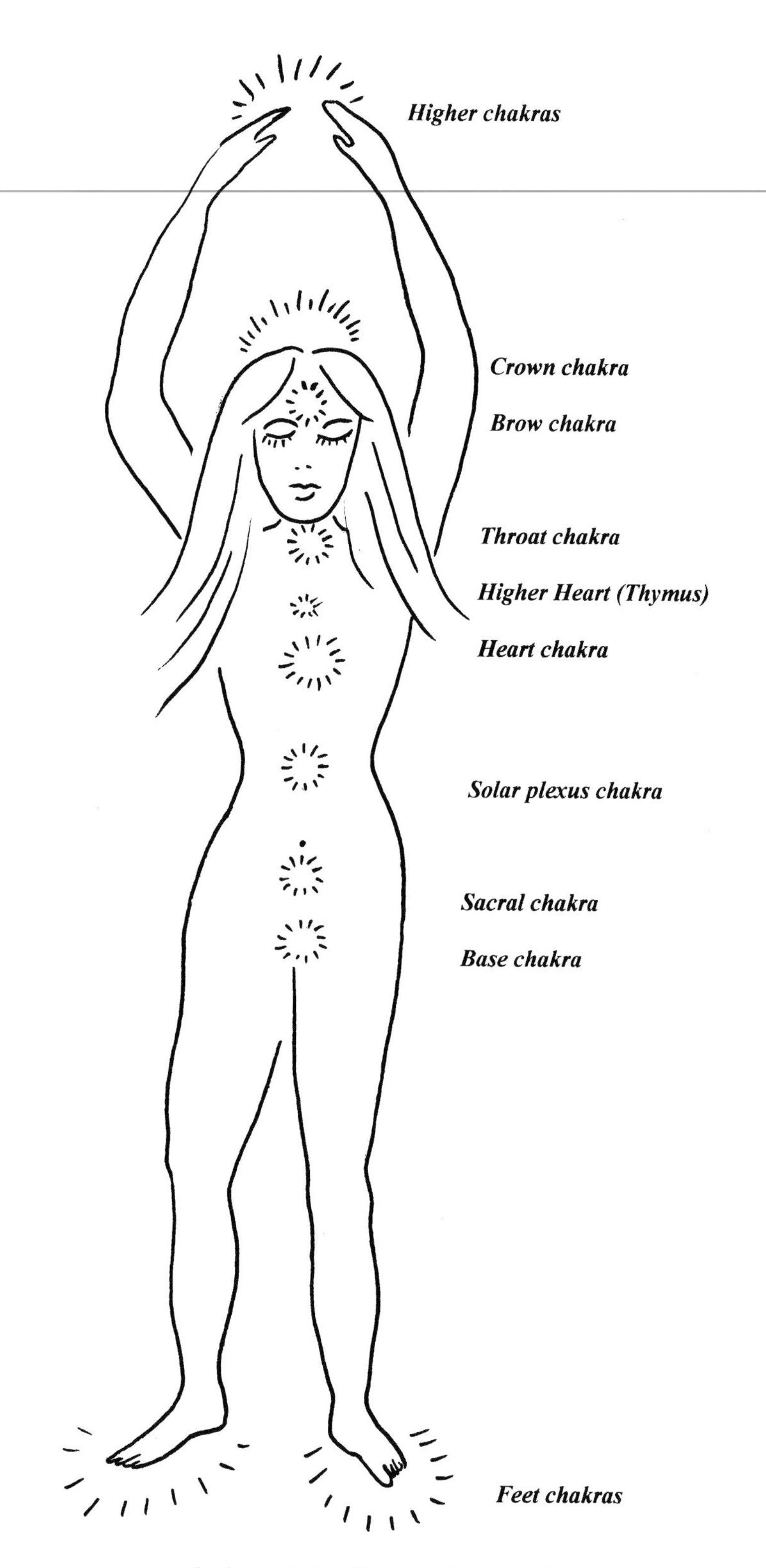

DIAGRAM OF THE CHAKRAS

BASE AND FEET CHAKRAS

Blocked/Unbalanced:
Spaced-out.
No vital energy.
Unreliable, impractical or accident prone.
Survival fears.
Dis-empowered.
Living in a dream world of future fantasies or past regrets.
Out of touch with feelings.
Unconscious 'avoidance' strategies.

Open/Balanced/Aligned:
Grounded & connected to Mother Earth.
Fully present.
Sense of purpose with the energy to get things done.
Manifesting one's vision in life and enjoying it fully.
'As above, so below', easier to link up with Higher Self to receive guidance and use it in a practical way.

SACRAL CHAKRA

Blocked/Unbalanced:
Blocked creativity.
Female issues.
Frustration, tension or impatience.
Emotional extremes.
Issues over intimacy &/or relationships.
Sexual issues with maybe guilt, repression or over-activity.
Often unhappy relationship with oneself.
Overworking, unbalanced need to achieve or hyperactive.

Open/Balanced/Aligned:
Happy in relationship with self & others.
Ability to 'go with the flow', grace & fluidity.
Creativity, patience, emotional security.

SOLAR-PLEXUS CHAKRA

Blocked/Unbalanced:
Over-Sensitivity.
Too open to the emotions, pains, fears of others, becoming overwhelmed & drained of energy.
Maybe unconscious need for attention with energetic 'cords'/'ties' with others, draining energy.
Dislike of being alone.
Can be power-control issues with insensitivity/or a 'doormat'.
Over-emotional & tearful.
Nervousness felt at solar-plexus.

Open/Balanced/Aligned:
Emotional balance with clear boundaries, yet sensitive to others' feelings.
Ability to say 'no' when necessary.
Emotional openness: can empathise without getting 'corded in' and feeling drained of energy.
Sense of self-worth, ability to value oneself fully.

HEART CHAKRA

Blocked/Unbalanced:
Fears.
Unforgiving nature.
Disillusionment.
Grudges, anger or ungrateful.
Grief & sorrow.
Jealousy.
Judgemental or critical.
Feeling life is 'unfair'.
Fear of closeness or intimacy.
Feelings of loneliness & isolation as one's ego builds barriers to 'protect' itself from being hurt emotionally.

Open/Balanced/Aligned:
Unconditional love, forgiveness, generosity of spirit.
Faith & trust in life.
Ability to 'know' & discern truth.
Gateway to Higher-Self: more peace, joy & happiness.
Spontaneity & enthusiasm – good to be around.
More kindness, compassion & understanding.

THROAT CHAKRA

Blocked/Unbalanced:
Suppressed emotions.
Inability to express one's true feelings or be oneself.
Blocked creativity.
False joviality.
Unable to express ones individuality, often due to karmic fears of repression or being different.
Self Consciousness &/or a Desire to 'Fit In'.
Often misunderstood by others.
Sudden emotional outbursts of pent up feelings.

Open/Balanced/Aligned:
Ability to speak ones truth in an open, honest way.
Ability to express emotions & how one really feels inside, rather than what others would like to hear.
No need to wear a false mask in a desire to be liked.
Loving communication & creative expression.

BROW CHAKRA

Blocked/Unbalanced:
Thoughts going round & round, with mental weariness & fatigue.
Disorientation, unable to focus mind & thoughts (see also base & solar-plexus).
Indecisive.
Frequently saying 'I don't know'.
Inability to see the bigger picture.
Overly rational approach to life.
Asking lots of questions.

Open/Balanced/Aligned:
Inner seeing, inner knowing & inner guidance.
Clear intuition and sense of certainty.
Less need for logical, 'left-brain' mental work when we intuitively perceive & 'know' the right answers.
Clear mind and clarity of thought. Uplifting.
More serenity, easier to meditate.

CROWN CHAKRA & HIGHER CHAKRAS

Blocked:
Little spiritual awareness or higher understandings.
Denial of a higher meaning of life.
No belief or knowing of our eternal state of being, thus a great fear of death - an energy pattern held by almost all humanity at the present time.
These fears are usually held in the lower chakras as the Crown resonates at a frequency where fear cannot exist.

Open/Balanced/Aligned:
More connection to ones soul & spiritual dimensions.
Spiritual wake-up call, connecting to higher realms.
For flying free - the freedom of a bird on the wing.
More connection to higher-self & I AM presence.
Deeper meditations & clearer guidance in dreams.

CHAKRAS & THE ETHERIC BLUEPRINT FOR WELL-BEING

Each Chakra relates to the Etheric Blueprint of the body in the area in which it is situated:

Base Chakra: Blueprint for lower body, legs & feet.
Sacral Chakra: Blueprint for the navel-abdomen-hip area.
Solar-Plexus Chakra: Blueprint for whole solar-plexus area.
Heart Chakra: Blueprint for the heart-chest area.
Throat Chakra: Blueprint for the neck-throat area.
Brow Chakra: Blueprint for the eyes-sinuses-forehead area.
Crown Chakra: Blueprint for the brain-head area.

Balancing/Strengthening the appropriate Chakra has a very positive effect on the etheric blueprint of the related area/s.

As we balance, open, clear & work on all the Lower Chakras, then everything else starts to fall into place.

See also Aotearoa Essences / www.nzfe.info
At Heartsong we also stock other NZ essences. See our website: www.heartsong.eu

COMBINATION ESSENCES FOR SELF-TREATMENT

As you can see with the Chakra Essences, combinations of flower and gem essences can be powerful tools for change and quick acting. It is therefore very easy to self-treat with these essences and also easy for the practitioner/healer to prescribe a combination which the client can take away with them to continue the healing process until the next session. Often people receiving a healing, Reiki or massage treatment can feel the effects and know it's doing them good, but they really appreciate something tangible, like an essence bottle to take from, something they can see that's 3D.

With the Eternal Light® System which I teach, I have found that many of those working with clients first try the essences on themselves, and when they have found how well they work, they then start to order them for clients. Out of all the practitioners I have trained, those that incorporate the essences with their work generally have the most success and faster, more consolidated results. (Of course not all workshop participants wish to work with others; many take Eternal Light® to help heal themselves and family).

OTHER FLOWER & GEM ESSENCES

At Heartsong we have over 500 different flower, gem or crystal essences, each with their own unique purpose for our healing, each given by the great Creator of all things.

Many of these essences have already been described in great detail in the Gurudas books (see recommended reading). These books were channelled in the '80s by Kevin Ryerson in America; Kevin is a very clear trance channel mentioned by Shirley McLaine in her books. Kevin channelled from John the apostle, who is now an Ascended Master on the higher dimensional planes. John (St Francis of Assisi, Kuthumi) has also been guiding me during many lifetimes and I have worked as a conscious channel for his energy to bring through information on other flower and gem essences, all of which are included in the Heartsong combinations and many of the Aotearoa essence plants.

I often make flower essences as I travel, Lotus in India, Californian essences, New Zealand essences and Mediterranean ones to name a few. Essences I was guided to make in Croatia all worked on war trauma and were used with great success in the refugee camps, alongside the healing methods I was teaching aid workers and refugees as part of my charity work there. Each essence has the energy not just of the flower or gem but the land it grows on.

With guidance a powerful anti-radiation combination has been formulated, which I have been invited to share and teach medical doctors in Chernobyl, Russia. The doctors there have run test trials on the essences and to also work with healing, as the allopathic medicine they work with is not healing the cause of the extremely high incidents of cancer and leukaemia since the nuclear 'accident' many years ago.

We have donated cases of mother tinctures and have trained the medical staff in their use and also to make their own essences.

There are photographs which are awe inspiring, taken at the clinic there, in my healing book, *Eternal Light*®. See Recommended Reading.

USING THE PHOTOGRAPHS FOR DIAGNOSIS

Each of you reading this book may intuitively know the essences you need in any given moment, simply by tuning into the beautiful colour photographs included in these pages.

There are several ways to use these diagnostic tools:

1). Sit quietly and meditate or still your mind. Ask inwardly 'which essence/s do I need now ?'. Then, staying in that quiet space, let the book fall open at the right page. The book and your higher-self will show you exactly what you need. Take a note of the page no. or picture, then ask internally if you need another and repeat.

Usually we will resonate with the essence when we read its healing purpose, but occasionally one will come up and we may think "that's not me, I don't need that one!" – TRUST WHAT YOU GET. We often cannot see all aspects of ourselves, or our ego chooses not to look at certain patterns we may hold. If in doubt, you can always ask a close friend or relative to give you a truthful answer.

2). Use each photograph as a meditation tool, for each picture carries it's unique energy, capturing the essence of the flower. You may also use the set of Bach flower cards from Heartsong to save damaging the book. As you stare at the flower, after a while close your eyes and imagine the flower's energy in your aura healing you. You will get a sense if you need the essence.

3). For the very sensitive, it can be enough to simply place your palm over the flower photograph and feel the energetic frequency coming from the aura of the flower.

4). For those so guided you may use the photographs to identify the living plants. Do remember though that there are many different types of some plants or trees and you will also need a very good botanical book to identify exactly the correct one.

Do not forget our unique individual attunement service for essence diagnosis. Please contact www.heartsong.eu for more information.

SEEING IS BELIEVING

Scientists are now finding ways to prove what seers have known throughout the ages, that subtle energy and auras exist. Kirlian photography shows the subtle energy field emanating from the hands, which, like the feet, give information and access points to the rest of the body. From these kirlian prints one can see where energy is balanced or where there are stressed organs to be worked on.

Likewise, with aura photography which shows the aura around head and shoulders in colour. These cameras are showing the subtle energy frequencies and translating them into colour via a computer. The results are certainly interesting. People at exhibitions have come to me to ask for information on themselves from those photos, as there is usually an aura photography stand at complementary therapy or esoteric shows. I have asked them not to show me the photo, looked at their aura clairvoyantly and given some knowledge, maybe, you have an energy leak on the left side of the throat chakra and the colours you are working with are predominantly......... etc. This is usually confirmed in the photo.

The three photographs shown here are proving how one can see energy and vibrational medicine working, in this case flower essences.

In the first photograph, Valerie's picture was taken to show her state of equilibrium at the time, before taking any flower essences. The photograph shows her to be very fuzzy and not very coherent, which in this system means blockages or physical illness.

In the second photograph, Valerie is only holding a bottle containing a combination of flower essences which I had diagnosed for her. The result as she simply holds the energy is extremely interesting. The energetic frequency in the bottle is causing quite a shift in Valerie's energy field as her subtle bodies try to come to terms with these new vibrations. It appears that she has split into two and it can just be seen that in the middle of her head, where it divides into two, is another energy, what appears to be a face. It looks to me to be a child's face, which could be symbolic of Valerie's inner child which still needed healing, or it could be a spirit or guide. Remember, at this stage, Valerie still has not taken even one drop of the flower essence she is holding.

The third photograph is taken 10 minutes after Valerie has taken one dose, four drops of the essence combination. Now, she has become aligned, centred and very coherent. This does not mean that she does not need to take any more of the essences. To the contrary, it is showing that this was the exact choice of essences for her at that time and she needs to take them regularly until those negative states being treated become permanently positive and totally healed.

The system used for these photographs is one of the most advanced forms of subtle energy diagnosis available. The system was invented by Patrick Richards and consists of a device called a Null Field Generator which allows a system termed VRIC (Visual Reference of Image Coherence), to be used as a method of assessment.

1.

2.

3.

Valerie Willmott

RECOMMENDED READING

Beyond Reiki – Eternal Light® by Shimara Kumara. Pub. Heartsong
ISBN. 978-0-9531533-1-2.

Bach and Karmic Flower Cards. by Shimara Kumara. Pub. Heartsong.
ISBN. 978-0-9531533-4-3

Healing the Inner Child Cards by Shimara Kumara. Pub. Heartsong.
ISBN. 0-9531533-2-0.

Flower Essences and Vibrational Healing by Gurudas. Cassandra Press Pub. Co., San Raphael CA. ISBN. 0-945946-04-X.

Gem Elixirs and Vibrational Healing, Volume 1 by Gurudas. Cassandra Press Pub. Co., San Raphael CA. ISBN. 0-961587-50-4.

The Collected Writings of Edward Bach edited by J Barnard. Flower Remedy Program. ISBN. 0-9506610-2-3.

An Astrological Study of the Bach Flower Remedies by P. Damian. Pub. C.W. Daniel. ISBN. 0-85435-195-7.

Love is Letting Go of Fear by Gerry Jampolski. Pub. Celestial Arts.
ISBN. 0-89087-246-5.

A Return to Love by Mariane Williamson. Pub. Aquarian/Thorsons.
ISBN. 1-855382571-00799.

A Course in Miracles Foundation for Inner Peace. Pub. Arkana.
ISBN. 0-14-019088-0-90301.

Heartsong Publications & Essences
PO Box 252
Totnes
Devon
TQ9 9DT, England

Tel. 01364 72112

All essences described in this book and many others, beautiful meditation CDs, Divine organic perfume, facial cream, sprays, catalogues and other books by Shimara are available to purchase on our website: www.heartsong.eu